D1348286

CITIZEN

BRANDS

Putting society at the heart of your business

MICHAEL WILLMOTT

JOHN WILEY & SONS, LTD

Chichester · New York · Weinheim · Brisbane · Singapore · Toronto

Other Wiley Editorial Offices

John Wiley & Sons, Inc., 605 Third Avenue,
New York, NY 10158-0012, USA

WILEY-VCH GmbH, Pappelallee 3,
D-69469 Weinheim, Germany

John Wiley & Sons Australia, 33 Park Road, Milton,
Queensland 4064, Australia

John Wiley & Sons (Asia) Pte Ltd, 2 Clementi Loop #02-01,
Jin Xing Distripark, Singapore 129809

John Wiley & Sons (Canada) Ltd, 22 Worcester Road,
Rexdale, Ontario M9W 1L1, Canada

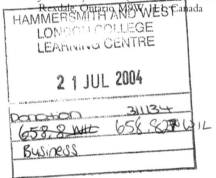

British Library Cataloguing in Publication Data
A catalogue record for this book is available from the British Library

ISBN 0-471-49212-4

Typeset in 11.5/15 Bembo by Florence Production Ltd, Stoodleigh, Devon
Printed and bound in Great Britain by Biddles Ltd, Guildford and King's Lynn

This book is printed on acid-free paper responsibly manufactured from
sustainable forestry, in which at least two trees are planted for each one
used for paper production.

For my friends at the Future Foundation
without whom this would not have been possible

CONTENTS

ACKNOWLEDGEMENTS

I am deeply indebted to many people who have helped in various ways in the development and production of this book.

First are all my colleagues at the Future Foundation who have helped to create the intellectual environment and cauldron of ideas that this book has so heavily drawn upon. These include Charlotte Grimshaw, who co-authored *The Responsible Organisation* with Melanie Howard and myself, and whose research and writing for that title contributed greatly to the historical perspective discussed in Chapter 3. In a similar vein, Sarah Graham worked with me and contributed to the analysis of the research on corporate citizenship conducted jointly with Richmond Events and Consumers' Association, to which I refer in a number of places in the book, particularly in Chapter 2. In a different area, Billy Nelson and Charlotte Cornish have been deeply involved in the work at the Future Foundation on choice and complexity that helped inform my analysis of these issues in Chapter 7.

Ben Hourahine worked as my editorial assistant in the final stages of the project, while Alexandra Denye has provided emotional and management support throughout. Finally, amongst my colleagues, a special mention must go to Michael Campbell who has not only helped me to understand complex system models, but also provided the simulations that are produced in Chapter 10.

Future Foundation associate Jim Murphy has shown me the need for, and benefits of, always questioning the status quo and received wisdom. A classic example is Jim's idea of 'peace and plenty' – which refutes the proposition of social and economic decline – that I discuss in some depth and give my own personal views on in Chapter 5.

Paul Ormerod introduced me to the whole area of complex system models and 'butterfly economics' and provided many of the research references in Chapter 10. Deborah Parkes from Richmond Events initiated the project on corporate citizenship mentioned above and provided objective comment and criticism throughout. She also suggested involving Consumers' Association as research partners and joint funders. In the two years that the programme ran, Paul Flatters and Leslie Sopp, who were at the time both at Consumers' Association, were fellow researchers and analysts whose contribution was extremely helpful.

The most instrumental person in the evolution of this book was my commissioning editor at Wiley's, Claire Plimmer. It was Claire who approached me with the idea that a book on this subject might be worth doing, and who has encouraged me throughout. Without her, this book would not have happened – I hope her judgement, and faith in me, were right.

Equally, without Bob Tyrrell's and David Darton's faith in me, and their invitation to join them at the Henley Centre, it is unlikely that I would ever have got into the forecasting and trend analysis business. But their influence on me over the years has been much more than that. They showed me how to look at and analyse consumer and other trends, how to assess their impact on business, and, most importantly, how to think creatively about the future.

I always received good advice from my father, Peter. He taught me the importance of objectivity in analysis. 'Where are the facts?'

he would always say when I had put some new analytic conclusion before him. As he did for many others, he helped me to improve my writing tremendously and I am sure would have made many useful comments on this book had he been alive. My mother, Phyllis, has been of similar help over the years, not least in commenting on my prose. An author and social historian, she has been hugely influential on my views on, and analysis of, the world.

But there are two people to whom I am most indebted for the opportunity to write this book. First is Melanie Howard, my co-founder of the Future Foundation. I have worked with Melanie for over ten years and many of the ideas that are put forward in this book have developed as a result of our joint work and her creative input into that. She unselfishly encouraged me to take on the task of writing the book and supported me throughout the process.

Last, but not least, is my wife, Marianne. She has endured my late nights, uneven moods and much else, both over the years and during the course of this project in particular. And most of the time she has done it with good humour, while always being a pragmatic, realistic and intelligent critic.

All these people have helped me greatly and, without them, I could not have completed this book. I hope it does not disappoint them.

INTRODUCTION
....

About ten years ago, I became interested in the broader
role and responsibilities of business in society – what was then,
and still is, referred to as corporate social responsibility. Over the
years, my views developed and I began to recognize that it was
more than just about companies 'doing good' – it also impinged
on key strategic and marketing issues like reputation and branding.
It was with this in mind that I first coined the phrase 'citizen
brands' in a 1997 report on corporate responsibility for British
Telecom.[1] Since then, whenever I have used it in conference
presentations or at client meetings, the term has proved to be a
popular one – for many people, it seems it epitomizes a new and
different approach to business.

Yet, during the course of writing this book, my ideas about
what exactly citizen brands stands for and why it is important have been shifting subtly. Whereas originally I used the term
to refer to the *responsibilities* that companies had in the wider

society, now I use it more broadly to describe the *relationship*[2] between a company and society. I now believe it to be even more important than I previously thought – indeed, given the trends in the world, one of the most critical issues facing business.

Yet, ask business leaders and management consultants what they think is the most important challenge facing companies today and they are unlikely to highlight this issue. Rather, they would identify globalization, new technology, supply chain management, e-commerce, regulation, core competencies, staff retention, price competition or the now popular innovation.

Important though all these are – and to different degrees to different companies in different sectors – they need to be considered alongside a new issue, a new dimension, which is emerging in the technological, globalized, knowledge economy ahead. This concept of *citizen brands* is one whose importance arises because it embodies not just one, but three crucial strategic issues for the business world: *branding, core values* and *corporate citizenship*. I believe that companies that understand and embrace this idea will be the ultimate winners in the future; those that do not face the risk of a bleak time ahead.

This book describes what I mean by citizen brands and presents the ever-mounting evidence that it is a vital aspect of business success, the processes at play that make it so important and what it implies for business behaviour and strategy.

MORE THAN CORPORATE RESPONSIBILITY

This book is not, however, just about corporate responsibility. Indeed, I believe there are good reasons for getting away from the traditional way that corporate responsibility has been defined and discussed. For a start, the term conjures up a vision of paternalism or 'do-gooding'. Corporate responsibility is therefore often viewed as an add-on to the core business strategy that companies are exhorted and expected to do simply because there are problems in the world and because companies have a responsibility, an obligation, to contribute, to give something back to society.[3]

While I am sympathetic to this view (there are indeed problems in the world that companies just should not ignore), we should recognize that this can be viewed as a sort of politicization by stealth. Certainly, proponents of corporate responsibility often do believe there are social, economic or environmental problems that companies should (with the perceived retreat of the welfare state) help to combat. Well-intentioned as this undoubtedly is, it clearly irritates some people in the business world, not least because there is often a self-righteousness about it which bears a resemblance to the philanthropic, paternal and moral corporate responsibility of Victorian industrialists that I outline in Chapter 3.

Many may disagree with my interpretation, but it results, at least in part, from my conversations and interviews with business leaders (and those advising business leaders) over the last few years. Rightly or wrongly, corporate responsibility has come to be seen by a significant number of people, including corporate managers, business analysts and political commentators, as self-righteous, politically motivated, do-gooding. The reaction from many is to re-emphasize the purpose of companies as being principally to generate profits for their shareholders.

I think we need to get away from this rather sterile debate. Three things are needed. First, I suggest the use of the term 'corporate citizenship' in place of corporate responsibility when describing the role of companies in society. Some might feel this a semantic point but it is in fact important. The very phrase 'corporate citizenship' suggests a more reciprocal and less philanthropic relationship – something that is certainly consistent with the more general notion of citizen brands.

BEYOND BENEFACTION

Second, it is important that corporate citizenship is recognized as being more than *benefaction*. Again, there is nothing wrong with benefaction. From the beginning of time people have acted charitably. Many give time or money to individual people, or to causes, on the basis of their moral or ethical beliefs. There is no reason why companies should not do the same (although companies as collections of individuals and work units may have more complicated decisions to make about what causes to support). It is likely that corporate benefaction will increase in the future as people become more aware and more concerned about a range of issues. But it seems to me wrong to equate benefaction with corporate citizenship, which is deeper, more involved, more reciprocal.

Corporate citizenship is not so much about a company 'giving' to charity (benefaction), although, of course, it might do that; it is much more about a company showing that it understands societal issues and cares about them.

Thus the distinction I am making between benefaction and citizenship is that the first is about responsibility, the second about a relationship; the first about ethics, the second about (social) values and interdependence.

REAPPRAISING VALUES

The third imperative is a reappraisal of the link between corporate citizenship, values and branding. In *Built to Last*[4] James Collins and Jerry Porras not only produced one of the best business books of the last decade but also highlighted the importance of core values to corporate success. How does the concept of citizen brands differ? It does so in two ways. First, I specifically link core values to corporate citizenship. For example, Collins and Porras argue that Phillip Morris is successful because it has a deeply embedded core ideology, even though the authors themselves do not (as they understatedly put it) see 'Philip Morris as working altruistically for the good of humankind'! They add:

> We concluded that the critical issue is not whether a company has the 'right' core ideology or a 'likeable' core ideology but rather whether it *has* a core ideology.

While this may have been true in the past, I argue that it is becoming increasingly unsustainable as the consuming public becomes more aware of social and ethical issues and more demanding of companies (see Chapter 2). For example, research I conducted in Britain[5] shows that when asked what adjectives (from a list of 30) best describe Marlboro, Philip Morris's main brand, the top six chosen by respondents were cynical, ruthless, heartless, secretive, deceitful and greedy. Philip Morris may have a strong ideology (the right to personal freedom and choice) but such negative views suggest a position that may well be unsustainable in the long term.

My second point of difference over *Built to Last* is that, whereas Collins and Porras's book concentrates on the internal impact of core values, I look specifically at the external impact – how the social values and behaviour of a company affect its branding and the way it is perceived by those outside the organization, particularly its customers. This is significant because branding is becoming more important in the high-tech, interconnected world of the future (the 'network society' as Manuel Castells has labelled it).[6]

THE MEANING OF CITIZEN BRANDS

Thus, three critical issues facing business today – corporate citizenship, core values and branding – come together in an integrated way to form the concept of citizen brands. Each is an important

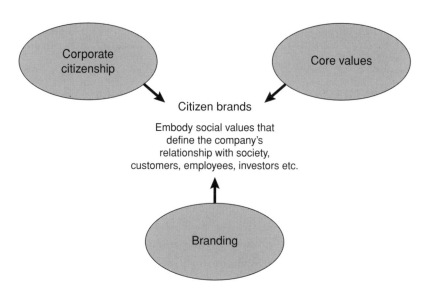

Figure I.1   Citizenship, values and branding.
Source: Michael Willmott/Future Foundation.

topic in its own right worthy of serious consideration by management. Together, they define a company's relationship with its customers, workers, owners and society in general (see Figure I.1). And in the emerging networked, post-industrial world, managing this relationship is surely the most important challenge facing companies.

My argument is predicated on two interrelated views. First, that citizen brands will become more commercially successful in the future. If this is not so, it will be extremely difficult to persuade companies to embrace the concept. Second, that wider concerns and ethical awareness are going to increase affecting people's views of companies as suppliers of goods and services, as employers and as owners of their capital (through direct share ownership or through indirect means like pension funds).

STRUCTURE OF THE BOOK

The book is structured with these points in mind. In the next chapter I present some of the case study and other evidence to support the thesis that citizen brands are successful brands. I follow this in Chapter 2 by considering consumer research, and specifically some of the Future Foundation's own surveys in this area. The aim here is to clarify why the issue is becoming more important in society (to people as consumers, employees, shareholders, suppliers and voters) and the ways in which it contributes to improved corporate performance. In Chapter 3, I discuss some of the barriers to current business action in this area and argue that there is less of a difference of opinion than people sometimes believe – based, in part, on an old-fashioned view of corporate responsibility. At the end of the first part of the book I describe the process by which being a citizen brand feeds through into commercial success – no mean task, as it is extremely difficult to prove definitively why and in what exact ways this process works (much as it is, for example, to prove that advertising works).

Whereas the first section of the book looks at the present – case studies of best practice, examples of successful action, evidence of the current debate and business and consumer opinion, and the process by which it all works – the second section looks to the future. A crucial part of my argument for the importance of citizen brands is that a number of social, technological, economic and consumer trends point to it becoming even more important in the future.

Chapter 5 looks at the emerging political economy and two aspects in particular: growing affluence in a post-cold-war environment ('peace and plenty') and the seemingly unstoppable process of globalization. In subsequent chapters I consider five specific trends that are particularly important:

- Technology and the implications for transparency, communications and network effects (such as word-of-mouth),
- The role of branding in a world where consumers' choices are expanding to the extent that they are almost 'drowning' in choice,
- The growth in scares, hysteria and the emergence of a 'culture of fear'[7] – a specific consequence of 'peace and plenty', that exposes all companies to shocks, panics and crisis management,
- The increase in consumer cynicism and towards multinational companies in particular,
- The development of more volatile and unpredictable consumer behaviour – the emergence of 'butterfly consumers'.

The final chapter of the book summarizes the key issues from earlier chapters and also considers the implications for business in terms of the challenges ahead and the broad strategies to adopt.

THE CASE FOR
CITIZEN BRANDS

CHAPTER 1

THE CASE FOR CITIZEN BRANDS

What do Hewlett Packard, Richard Branson's Virgin and British retailer Marks and Spencer have in common? Not a lot one would have thought. They operate in different industries, on different scales, with different geographical coverage and with different current levels of commercial health.

Hewlett Packard is an IT company that is currently 'reinventing' itself under new CEO Carly Fiorina. Its stock has underperformed the market since 1999 and in November 2000 it had to call off the prospective acquisition of PricewaterhouseCoopers' consulting arm following disappointing fourth quarter results. Richard Branson's Virgin Group operates in a range of sectors including airlines, trains, music, mobile telephony and financial services. In December 1999 it sold a minority stake in its Virgin Atlantic airline to Singapore Airways for £600 million – a figure 'far more than most analysts had thought it worth'.[1] At the moment Virgin appears to be going from strength to strength.

Marks and Spencer, the best known name in British retailing, is on the other hand having a torrid time. The last two years have been riddled with profit warnings, disappointing results and a collapse in share price.

So what do these three companies have in common? Well, in their different ways they are examples of citizen brands. They are not perfect examples, but then I am not sure that any company yet is. But the values they encompass explain Virgin's current success, why HP will continue to prosper in the hi-tech sector in the twenty-first century and why Marks and Spencer is likely to once again be a leading player in the British high street (unless it is acquired by another company that fails to embrace, and build on, its core values).

Their stories are all different but they all have one thing in common – a strong set of core values that relate to their roles in, and relationships with, society. And the reason for being optimistic, rather than pessimistic, about their future prospects is strong evidence that those values and those relationships provide a sound base from which to build success. For a whole range of studies has shown that, on the whole, being a good citizen does, indeed, equate to commercial success.

THE EVIDENCE

Organizations like Business for Social Responsibility and The Business Enterprise Trust in the United States or the Centre for Tomorrow's Company and Business in the Community in Britain have summarized some of the studies in this area. Their conclusions are clearcut.

For example, the Centre for Tomorrow's Company – whose own particular formulation of corporate responsibility initiatives it calls the 'inclusive approach' – has argued that:

At the very least, the research supports the view that the inclusive approach, while serving shareholders' interests, particularly in the long-term, does lead to business success as a result of improved customer satisfaction, greater commitment on the part of employees, a more effective supply chain, and an enhanced reputation in the community at large.[2]

While, in the United States, Business for Social Responsibility has noted that:

Over the past decade, a growing number of companies have recognized the business benefits of CSR [corporate social responsibility] policies and practices. Their experiences are bolstered by a growing body of empirical studies which demonstrate that CSR has a positive impact on business economic performance, and is not harmful to shareholder value.[3]

A Committee of Inquiry that reported to the British Government, came to the same conclusion (as have others who looked at the evidence):

The evidence [stacks up] to the point where any reasonable person must begin to ask what more might be required to demonstrate a binding cause and effect relationship between increased competitiveness and environmentally and socially responsible behaviour.[4]

Although there is no reason to doubt the conclusions of these bodies, it was necessary for the purposes of this book to consider some of the specific studies themselves not least because the umbrella title of *citizen brands* includes such a diverse range of issues. But before discussing the specifics, there are some general observations to make as a result of my analysis of the research:

1. A number of these studies and research projects are, in fact, consumer surveys, many of them attitudinal. These are notoriously difficult to interpret particularly when they are of the form 'I would pay 10% more for an environmentally friendly product' or 'other things being equal, I would choose a company that is

socially responsible'. This does not mean that they should be discarded as such but rather that they should be treated in a different way and separately from studies based on more direct commercial measures such as share price performance or profitability. For example, some researchers have looked at the correlation between environmentally friendly practices and profitability; others at the relationship between executive pay and share price. It is for this reason that I consider the consumer research in a separate chapter.

2. When you take out these consumer research analyses, there are fewer direct attempts to assess the impact of corporate citizenship on business performance than might be imagined. However, as I show in this chapter, when the results of these studies are considered together, they do provide a consistent, and I believe persuasive, argument in support of the citizen brands thesis.

3. Interestingly, and importantly, there are very few studies that show the converse − that is, that being a citizen brand is bad strategically and commercially. Given the opposition that exists in some quarters to the idea, I believe this, in itself, lends support to the citizen brand argument. Where there is criticism of some initiatives in this area they tend to be of the values and motives involved (altruism versus self-interest) rather than the effect (that citizenship is good for the company). An example is a paper by Joel Schwartz of the Hudson Institute[5] where he argues that corporate philanthropy is acceptable if it is driven by self-interest but not if it is the result of altruism ('corporate philanthropy cannot really be justified unless its motive is "impure"').

4. All the studies that have been conducted are, inevitably, backward looking. Some of them, limited by the availability of data, have been forced to look at relationships existing in the early 1990s or even the 1980s. Since part of my argument is that the concept of citizen brands is becoming more important

it is likely, therefore, that the relationship between citizenship and commercial success will strengthen in the future (and perhaps be easier to measure and prove). This is why I devote the second part of the book to looking at this aspect.

With these points in mind, what exact evidence is there of a relationship between citizenship and commercial success? Here, I summarize the results of over 30 different studies on a variety of different aspects.

For sake of clarity I have classified the research projects into six different categories, some more general, others more specific:

- governance
- values, ethics and culture
- employment
- community
- environment
- investors.

GOVERNANCE

The starting point for assessing how well a company is likely to manage its relationships with the rest of society, is how well it manages itself. That this is an issue not only for the wider populace but for business too is evident from the string of Committees set up to address corporate governance issues in Britain in the 1990s. First Cadbury, then Greenbury (specifically on executive pay) and finally the Hampel Committee in 1997/98 all recognized that there were areas where companies could do better in corporate governance. But, as far as I can tell they have had little impact. (Indeed, some argued at the time that Hampel in particular missed a 'golden opportunity' to be bolder.[6]) A recent PIRC report presented, according to the *Financial Times*, 'a grim picture of the state of corporate governance in boardrooms. Just 17 per cent of companies were found to be fully compliant with the City's own combined code of best practice, introduced two years ago.'[7] This is strange as a number of studies have demonstrated the importance of good corporate governance. A study in the *McKinsey Quarterly*[8] found that three-quarters of the 200 institutional investors asked felt that board practices were at least as important as financial performance when evaluating investments. More than this, the respondents said they were prepared to pay around 20 per cent more for shares of a well-governed company. It seems that good corporate governance helps to support the share price.

Nowhere is the issue of corporate governance more topical than in the area of executive pay. Excessive executive pay has achieved unfavourable headlines on both sides of the Atlantic. It is an emotive issue and one that is likely to continue to be so. In the United States, Chief Executives of top companies earned 106.9 times more than the average worker in 1999. In 1965 it was 20.3 times. As *The State of Working America* put it 'In 1999, a US CEO worked half a week to earn what an average worker earned in 52 weeks. In 1965, by contrast it took a CEO two and a half weeks to earn a workers' average annual pay'.[9] What is surprising though, is that paying your executives excessive amounts is not only questionable on ethical grounds but on commercial ones too.

Research at the Wharton business school comparing CEO compensation and financial performance over one, three and five years, showed that companies that pay their chief executives too much typically perform badly in terms of profits and share price.[10] Good governance, good Board conduct, should, therefore, try to ensure that boardroom pay is kept within reasonable bounds.

One final point on executive pay is the link between it and being a citizen brand. A study by Ahmed Riahi-Belkaoui[11] found that in America in the 1980s there was a negative correlation between 'external perceptions of social performance' (rating of a company by fellow industry specialists on its responsibility to community/environment) and managers' pay. This led the author to conclude that it 'suggests that executives may be penalized for such activities'. There is another possible interpretation though. If, successful companies are, as I will show in this book, more likely to have a higher social performance (as Riahi-Belkaoui puts it), and successful companies do not provide excessive pay, as the Wharton research found, then you would expect a negative correlation. Whether this was the explanation for the result in the 1980s remains to be seen – I am sure it will be the case in the future. Excessive executive pay and being a citizen brand do not sit happily together.

VALUES, ETHICS AND CULTURE

The debate about governance leads naturally on to the issue of values, ethics and culture. Here, a whole host of studies have shown the link between a culture that embraces citizenship in some form or other and commercial success. In terms of values, the critical thing seems to be having those that are clearly defined and particularly those that are inclusive. As I noted in the Introduction, James Collins and Jerry Porras, in their book *Built to Last*, found clear values and inclusiveness to be among the common qualities of long-lasting US companies, and that there was a clear correlation between these qualities and above average stock market performance.

Kotter and Heskett studied 200 companies over 20 years and also found superior long-term profitability was associated with corporate cultures that express the company's purpose in terms of all stakeholder relationships.[12] A recent Harvard University study showed that 'stakeholder-balanced' companies generated four times the growth rate and eight times the employment growth of companies that are focused solely on shareholders.[13]

Similarly, an attention to ethical principles and behaviour has benefits. Business for Social Responsibility[14] has noted for example that 'a recent 1999 study, cited in *Business and Society Review*, showed that . . . companies which made a public commitment to rely on their ethics codes outperformed companies that did not do so by two or three times, as measured by market value added'. And, that in 'a 1997 DePaul University study companies with a defined commitment to ethical principles do better financially (based on annual sales/revenues) than companies that do not'.

A good example of a company with strong, inclusive values is Hewlett Packard. In 1949, David Packard, co-founder of HP, made the point clearly:

> I suggested that . . . management people had a responsibility beyond that of making a profit for their stockholders. I said that we . . . had a responsibility to our employees to recognize their dignity as human beings.[15]

Another part of HP's core values as defined by Packard was that the company existed 'first and foremost to make a contribution to society'.[16] This Hewlett Packard 'way' is alive and well today. Although, of course, she puts it somewhat differently, new Chief Executive Officer Carly Fiorina makes the same points 50 years later:

> A leader's greatest obligation is to make possible an environment where people's minds and hearts can be inventive, brave, human and strong, where people can aspire to do useful and significant things, where people can aspire to change the world.
>
> At Hewlett-Packard we call this way of thinking, this set of behaviors, the rules of the garage. You see the garage is a special place to us; it is where we began. But these rules are about the way we compete and the way we work.[17]

Note that this company competes, but it does it in a way that is built around and on the skills of its people and with the aim of changing the world. Compare that to Britain's Barclays Bank which faced a barrage of negative publicity as it closed branches during 2000 while running an advertising campaign that emphasized its size and international credentials. According to an internal report leaked to the *Sunday Times* newspaper, Barclays was seen as having a 'culture of greed' and that being big was equated with 'not caring'.[18]

The impact of a company's ethics and values is apparently very important for recruitment. In a recent KPMG survey four out of five employees who thought their managers would keep to ethical standards would recommend the company to potential recruits compared to only one in five who did not have this faith in their managers.[19]

EMPLOYMENT

How companies treat their people – their employees – is an important part of being a citizen brand. Here again, all the research shows the commercial benefits of being a good employer.

A number of recent studies have reinforced the intuitively obvious point that employee-focused companies are more profitable. In *Frontiers of Excellence*, Robert Waterman concluded: 'Companies that set profits as their No. 1 goal are actually less profitable in the long run than people-centred companies'.[20] A 1999 Watson Wyatt Worldwide survey of 400 companies found that those with more 'employee friendly' policies had higher returns for shareholders: 103 per cent over five years for the best employers to 53 per cent for the worst.[21] And another study found that the companies people would most like to work for outgrew others by a four to one margin, were more profitable and created more jobs.[22]

The point is reinforced by the experience of UK Investors in People companies who outperform the national average on a range of financial measures (see Table 1.1).[23]

Table 1.1 Investing in people works

Performance measure	National average	IIP average
Return on capital employed	9.38%	18.93%
Pre-tax profit margin	3.03%	4.67%
Sales per employee	£77 447	£122 108

Source: RSA Inquiry *Tomorrow's Company*, 1995.

Good employment strategies have an impact on the share price too (see also investors below). In Germany, Linda Bilmes, Konrad Wetzker and Pascal Xhonneux's analysis of more than 100 companies revealed a strong link between investing in employees and stock market performance. Companies that place workers at the core of their strategies produce higher long-term returns to shareholders than their industry peers do.[24] At the other end of the scale, getting rid of staff – the downsizing that was so prevalent in the 1990s – is *not* associated with a better stock market performance, according to a Watson Wyatt study. And, a University of Colorado research exercise showed that downsizing does not lead to increased profits either.[25] Indeed, as Gary Hamel and C.K. Prahalad noted in their influential book *Competing for the Future*, share prices might even lag behind competitors after a downsizing:

> The study concluded that a savvy investor should look at a restructuring announcement as a signal to sell rather than buy.[26]

Perhaps one reason why downsizing fails to improve the commercial performance of companies is that it undermines staff spirit ('the inevitable result of downsizing is plummeting employee morale' as Hamel and Prahalad put it) and this feeds directly through to customer satisfaction.

The work of Bain & Co shows that those companies that have the highest employee retention have the greatest customer retention (Figure 1.1). Since those companies that have the best

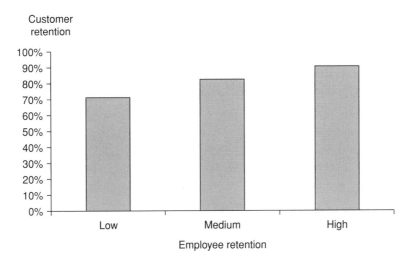

Figure 1.1   Employee and customer retention. Branch banking in Europe.

Source: Bain & Co.

customer retention also have the highest profitability it is clear how the connection is made.

Eli Lilly's research among its own staff indicated, as CEO Randall L. Tobias put it, 'very clearly and very convincingly that employee and customer satisfaction are strongly and positively linked'.[27] Lilly is a company that takes its employees (and indeed its relationship with all society) very seriously. So too does Hewlett Packard which, according to a new book, has built up a 'bank of emotional resilience' among its people.[28] This is one reason why, HP epitomizes a citizen brand more than most.

With the process of globalization, companies increasingly have to be attentive to employment practices throughout their supply chain particularly where these involve developing nations. This is important because it can be much harder for companies to monitor standards and because (as I discuss in subsequent chapters) it can be the focus of considerable media attention (and consumer reproach). For example, British retailer Marks and Spencer, which is recognized as having a particularly inclusive and supportive approach to its staff, was accused by Indonesian workers' leaders of selling clothes made by child labourers at ludicrously low rates (50p for a 10 hour day).[29] The company denied the charge and now has a set of 'Global Sourcing Principles' and seems to have ridden out the storm. The reason it has done so, when others like Nike arguably have not, is I believe because it has built up a bank of goodwill by its past activities in a range of citizenship areas.

COMMUNITY

Marks and Spencer has a long tradition not only of being employee focused but, like a number of other retailers, of being heavily involved in local communities too. This helps to build its reputation and connectedness to society that is so crucial to being a citizen brand. But it has a direct and measurable impact on company performance as well. According to the *Independent* newspaper, Marks and Spencer's secondment of its staff to community projects 'produced an average competency gain of 29% over a range of skills, with greatest improvements in communication, project management, customer focus and decision-making'.[30] So this sort of community activity not only helps to build rapport with local people and reputation with it, but has human resource benefits too.

This result is mirrored in American research where a Council of Foundations report noted that employees involved in a business's community activities were 30 per cent more likely to continue working for the company.[31] British retailer Woolworths has invested heavily in local community initiatives with, to date, very promising results particularly in terms of staff motivation.[32]

Of course, in a global economy community initiatives can be global too. In October 2000 Hewlett Packard announced a $1 billion package of partner products and services under its World e-Inclusion programme. This aims to help the poor in the developing world benefit from new technology and e-services.

ENVIRONMENTAL ISSUES

Closely related to community initiatives are environmental ones. These too can either be local or global. This is an area where a lot of work has been carried out with nearly all of it showing the commercial benefits of environmental awareness.

For example, in May 1997 the *Guardian* reported that new research had shown that companies taking environmental issues seriously had better financial performances than that of their non-green rivals. The study from Imperial College and Jupiter Asset Management had 'found that a large sample of greener companies did as well as or better than competitors in the same business over a four year period.'[33] At about the same time, the *Financial Times* ran a headline 'Green is the colour of money' on a report about the 1997 Queen's Awards for Industry. It went on to say that 'the Queen's Awards for Environmental Achievement this year provide ample support for the thesis that helping the environment can help company profits too.'[34]

More specifically, ICF Kaiser, one of the United States' largest engineering consulting groups, discovered that companies that 'green' their corporate practices can make their shareholders up to 5 per cent richer. According to Kaiser, when risks are reduced by the introduction of responsible corporate environmental practices – and the improvements are communicated to Wall Street – companies become more attractive investments. The study found that

> Adopting a more environmentally proactive posture has, in addition to any direct environmental and cost-reduction benefits, a significant and favourable impact on the firm's perceived riskiness to investors and, accordingly, its cost of equity capital and value in the market place.[35]

In the same vein, Dow Chemical is one of a number of companies that has realized the commercial benefit of environmental policies.

> When Dow Chemical announced recently that it planned to invest $1bn (£645m) in new environmental equipment and programmes during the next ten years, the real news was not the size of the proposed expenditure but the company's prediction that it would make a return of between 30 and 40 per cent on its investment.[36]

Perhaps the most comprehensive analysis has been that of the US-based Alliance for Environmental Innovation which reviewed all the available studies in this area. They concluded:

> That out of the 70 studies, not a single one found a negative correlation between superior environmental performance and financial performance. These studies suggest that environmentally superior companies command a market place premium of 150 to 250 basis points.[37]

One final example comes from a rather different source. Ahmed Riahi-Belkaoui is a Professor of Accounting at the University of Illinois-Chicago. In his book *Corporate Social Awareness and Financial Outcomes* he takes a detached accountant's view of these issues. Here are his conclusions from the penultimate chapter of the book where he looks at pollution control and stock market performance by analysing data from 100 US companies:

> In fact, on the basis of these results, managers may be advised to allocate a proportion of their resources to pollution control and to report these expenditures to stockholders.[38]

In other words, the market on the whole rewarded the companies that spent money on pollution control mechanism and, importantly, disclosed this to stockholders. Being environmentally friendly made business sense.

INVESTORS

For investors then, whether a company is a citizen brand is a crucial piece of information. This raises two questions. What evidence is there that good corporate citizenship is related to an increased share price? And is this recognized by investors?

Clearly on the first point there are some specific examples where being a good citizen is not enough to maintain a company's position in the stock market – Marks and Spencer being a current high profile example of this. But, as I discuss below, this partly reflects other business issues – being a citizen brand on its own is not enough to guarantee success. But, evidence from specifically focused social, environmental or ethical funds – which by definition cover a broader range of companies – does suggest a link. The Social Investment Forum analysed the performance of socially responsible mutual funds and found that they had done well on both a one year and three year basis.[39] It quotes Wiesenberger, a Thomson Financial company, as finding that 25 out of the 46 social and environmental mutual funds were in the top quartile of their investment categories over three years (so over 50 per cent are in the top 25 per cent of all funds). Nine of the funds (20 per cent) are in the top 10 per cent.

In 1997, US academics Robert D. Klassen and Curtis P. McLaughlin assessed what happened to companies that won environmental awards and those that were involved in disasters like oil spills.[40] They found the positive news produced an average rise in share price of nearly 1 per cent, while a problem produced a fall of 1.5 per cent.

It is perhaps not surprising, therefore, that investors are increasingly taking account of citizenship issues, although there is clearly some way to go before it becomes universal. Critical in this will be the actions of investors themselves and their advisers. Evidence from both suggests a keen awareness of the issues. There is now, too, an obligation in Britain for pension fund trustees to define their attitude to 'socially responsible investment', as a result of the 1995 Pensions Act that came into force in July 2000.

A survey for the Prince of Wales Business Leaders' Forum sought the views of 100 institutional investors, regulators, parliamentarians, business journalists and non-governmental organizations in three European countries. Three-quarters felt that responsible social and environmental behaviour would increasingly affect a company's share price and only one in seven disagreed (presumably one in ten were undecided).[41]

As long ago as 1996, Kleinwort Benson was claiming that inclusive companies outperform the market – 'earnings per share is no longer the key measure . . . investors are more intent on finding out the sources of value' – and set up a new investment fund focusing on 'inclusive' companies. The *Financial Times* commented:

> Even accountants have begun to talk of adopting a 'balanced scorecard' in performance assessment and to describe relying on financial measures as 'driving while looking in the rear-view mirror'.[42]

And for a variety of reasons, pension funds are increasingly active in this area. As Will Hutton notes, in Britain 'there are now £2.6 billion of savings funds explicitly mandated to invest in companies who demonstrate social, environmental and ethical responsibility in their business policies'.[43] He goes on to point out that Britain's third largest pension fund – the Universities Superannuation Scheme – has made it clear it will confront poor environmental and ethical behaviour when managing its £20 billion of assets.

Clearly managers have a responsibility to take note of the wishes of the company's owners. If shareholders increasingly want companies to be better citizens then it is their duty to follow that instruction. It does not matter whether the motivation is an ethical/altruistic one (as might be the case with certain pension funds or individual investors) or a commercial one (where the shareholders recognize it is just good business practice) or a combination of the two. And you would have thought that investors will increasingly support citizenship initiatives as they recognize that being a good citizen is actually good for business.

PUTTING SOCIETY AT THE HEART OF BUSINESS

The concept of citizen brands brings together the three issues of values (what the company stands for), corporate citizenship (playing an active role in society) and branding (the tangible and intangible attributes that are encompassed in a name or trademark).[44] Taken together these define a company's relationship with all the relevant people and institutions it has to deal with.[45]

In an era when management consultants talk about putting the customer at the heart of the company, perhaps another way of describing the concept of citizen brands is of it being about *putting society at the heart of the company.*

If brands encapsulate values, intangible attributes and the relationship between a company and its customers (and society as a whole), then they are in effect social constructs. This is important for the companies and organizations that build and manage brands. Companies through their direct actions (for example employment) and through their intermediaries – brands – are an integral part of the social and economic world they operate in, needing to reflect the values and aspirations that exist; the differences and similarities. This is why corporate managers need to bring society into the company; why they need to turn their brands into citizen brands. At the most basic level, this is why all the research has found that good corporate citizenship is so strongly related to commercial success.

Companies like Body Shop, Ben and Jerry's, The Co-operative Bank, British Telecom or IBM all in different ways, and to different degrees, recognize this. So too do Hewlett Packard, Marks and Spencer and Virgin.

CITIZENSHIP IS NOT ENOUGH

People may be surprised by my choice of Hewlett Packard and Marks and Spencer as examples of citizen brands as they are both under something of a cloud at the moment. But this helps to emphasize an important point: *being a citizen brand alone is not enough*.

Just because a company is a good corporate citizen does not mean it can ignore some of the basic principles of sound management. Three things in particular are important: efficient production; superior quality; and customer focus. The point is that the most successful companies will combine citizenship with all these aspects.

Arguably, this is where Marks and Spencer went wrong and it demonstrates some of the conflicts that can arise from being a citizen brand. Marks and Spencer had always sourced much of its clothing range from British suppliers. But these were more expensive than foreign producers. For a while, Marks – as a good corporate citizen – kept with its local suppliers, but eventually, as its products fell behind on a value for money basis, it had to do something. The company only really had two options. First, which was suggested by some pundits, it could have made a point of its good citizenship credentials: 'pay a bit more because you are supporting British workers'. But, as a potential global player in a global economy, Marks decided (quite rightly in my view) that this was unsustainable and opted for the second option. This was to do what every other major clothing manufacturer does – source the product from overseas. This, of course, helps to create jobs in other, mainly developing, countries and, despite the criticism it sometimes receives, can in the right circumstances be seen as a positive act of corporate citizenship.[46]

Marks and Spencer's attachment to its local, British suppliers was an indication of a complacency within the company that arose out of its success. But it was also complacent about its customers

– it lost touch with what its market wanted. And if there is one danger that can arise from corporate citizenship it is that it can turn into paternalism and arrogance when the company is particularly successful. So, despite being a good corporate citizen Marks and Spencer lost the plot. But, and this is the important point, its behaviours and actions in the past, its inherent values, mean it retains a special position in British consumers' hearts. It has that bank of goodwill. Despite its poor recent performance it still has very high consumer ratings on critical citizenship issues as I show in the next chapter.

With a new management team in place that is taking a more proactive approach to its customer base and yet which retains the fundamental values that have been part of the business for many years the chances are that the company will re-establish itself.

Hewlett Packard's position is a more puzzling one. Having grown revenues and earnings every year for the last five years, its main problem seems to be that it is not as successful as some of its hi-tech competitors. In November 2000 it announced year-on-year revenue growth of 17 per cent yet disappointed the market by missing its earnings per share target. But this is a solid company and a good corporate citizen – it will be a surprise if it is not still a major player in years to come.

My final example – Virgin – is rather different. It does put its employees first and is very consumer focused but it does it in an unorthodox way. Richard Branson himself makes the point: 'Virgin Direct illustrates one of the great strengths of the Virgin Group: we thrive on *mavericks* [my emphasis]'.[47] It thrives on being different. 'To some traditionalists . . . the fact that Virgin has minimal management layers, no bureaucracy, a tiny board and no massive global HQ is an anathema'.[48] But most important of all in my view is the way Virgin positions itself so clearly as a consumer champion. It is one of us, it is a citizen, it is a citizen brand.

This positioning of Virgin, and its success, highlights an important point about being a citizen brand. As I show in the next chapter, the ideal citizen brand is not only sympathetic, trustworthy and friendly but also dynamic and innovative. Virgin's success – its connection with society – is based on its understanding of consumer needs, its innovation in addressing those and its determination to take on monopolistic or complacent competition. As I also show later, it is much easier to gain the benefits of being a citizen brand in more competitive markets than in less competitive ones. If Virgin has thrived on its dynamism in competitive markets, Marks and Spencer's current plight demonstrates the dangers of complacency that follow from market domination and the lack of innovation that can ensue.

Hewlett Packard, Marks and Spencer and Virgin are all brands that have something about them that is more than just an offer of good quality or service or value for money. That something comes from their internal values and their views about their roles and positions in the world. HP wants to make the world a better place, M&S wants a cohesive and prosperous community, Virgin to champion the consumer. They all, in their own different ways, epitomize some aspect of citizen brands. It is not a guarantee that they will succeed in the future, but it certainly gives them a head start.

BRANDS, CITIZENSHIP AND CONSUMERS

CHAPTER 2

BRANDS, CITIZENSHIP AND CONSUMERS

*I*f the last chapter provided case study and other evidence of the strategic and financial importance of being a citizen brand, this chapter concentrates on a range of consumer research studies. The aim here is to:

- Understand the wider concerns of consumers and citizens,
- Assess the extent to which this affects (if at all) their consumer decisions and their perceptions and expectations of companies,
- Investigate the process or relationship between the two.

In particular, I am going to draw on three pieces of research carried out by myself and my colleagues at the Future Foundation. The first was a project commissioned by British Telecom in 1997,[1] the second was some work conducted jointly with Richmond Events and Consumers' Association in 1998 and 1999,[2] while the third involves a special analysis of the Future Foundation's annual monitor of consumer attitudes carried out as part of its *n*Vision service.[3] To supplement this I call on other pieces of relevant consumer research as necessary.

ALTRUISM AND SELF-INTEREST?

My starting point is a fairly fundamental question – why are people concerned or worried about certain issues? Here, the research suggests that there are two, on the face of it contradictory, aspects to people's interest in issues like poverty, child welfare or the environment – one more self-centred, the other more altruistic.

Unsurprisingly, people will inevitably have some worries about those social and economic factors that might affect either themselves personally or those who are close to them, be they family, friends, work colleagues or acquaintances in the local community. Indeed, throughout history personal fears have arguably been the most important factor in the development of a whole range of political initiatives and particularly during the last two centuries as democracy has developed. The range of legislative, institutional and welfare mechanisms introduced from the middle of the nineteenth century to protect against, and counter, hardship, reflected the personal concerns that were evident during that time in such areas as basic health standards, poverty and working conditions. I discuss this further in the next chapter. Equally, I believe that a real fear about how global warming might directly affect people (or their descendants) was a major factor in the growth of environmentalism in the 1980s and 1990s. Current concerns and political responses show the same tendency (see, for example, my discussion of genetic engineering in Chapter 8).

Second are more altruistic concerns that are, or at least appear to be, born out of ethical or moral beliefs. For example, people may be worried about human rights or third world poverty, even though they, or people they know, are unlikely to be personally affected by them. An interest in animal rights or conservation in far-off lands is likely to be driven by a set of beliefs about what is right or wrong rather than a fear that these pose a direct threat to people's lives in the industrialized world.

Although these would seem to be clearly separate issues, they are, in fact, quite difficult to disentangle. The Future Foundation's 1997 research for British Telecom asked about both *general concerns* on a range of broad issues (which might be prompted by moral, ethical or political convictions on issues like third world poverty) and *personal worries* that people currently had (for example, local crime or losing their job at some point in the future). When compared to each other, there is a correlation between personal concerns and altruistic ones, as Figure 2.1 illustrates. Those aspects that people were most personally worried about were also the ones that they were generally concerned about too. So, for

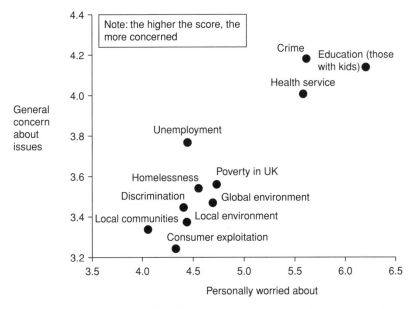

Figure 2.1 Altruism and self-interest. How concerned people are about different issues – mean scores.

Source: *The Responsible Organisation*, BT/Future Foundation.

example, in their day-to-day lives it is things like crime, the health service and education that most people are worried about. These also get the highest ratings as issues facing society generally.

To illustrate the point further, an analysis of different groups in society highlights how people's own specific circumstances will, not surprisingly, condition the issues that they are personally concerned about. For example:

- Women who are not working are more concerned about the local community (50 per cent higher than the total population) clearly because they spend more time in it (and are more likely either to have children or be elderly making them more dependent on local amenities and services).
- Parents with school age children are more concerned about education.
- Those in society who have suffered most from redundancy in the last few decades are more concerned about unemployment. The proportion of middle-aged manual workers who are worried about this is nearly a third higher than the population as a whole.[4]

This is not to say that altruistic concerns do not exist. The British Telecom study found that a significant minority of the population (around 10 per cent) was extremely concerned about specific ethical issues like human rights, fair trade or third world poverty. (These issues are not included in Figure 2.1 as respondents were not asked whether they were worried that they might be personally affected by them – for the simple reason that very few people in Britain are likely to be so. Most people do not, for example, have relatives living in the third world, let alone suffering from poverty or exploitative labour practices. Nor do many have friends or family living under human rights abusing regimes. Certainly, there are not enough to generate sufficient responses in a standard sized sample survey.) The study also found that slightly more than a third of the population could be classified as having a generally ethical outlook on life. These people say they are very or extremely concerned about a whole group of broad issues ranging from animal rights, to third world poverty to global and local environmental problems. While, in part, this is clearly a consequence of personality and outlook on life it is also the case that those in professional and managerial occupations and in higher income groups are more likely to have an 'ethical' stance. Personal circumstance, in terms of greater affluence and higher occupational status, plays its part too it seems.

The conclusion from the British Telecom research was that although there is a complex interaction making it difficult to determine how much an individual's concern about an issue is driven by personal fears or more broadly-based altruism, these two underlying dimensions do exist. And, important though both dimensions are, it is the personal, non-altruistic aspect that is currently the most influential. Two further conclusions arising from the importance of personal circumstances and fears are, in the context of this book, perhaps more important.

First, this 'personalization of altruism' creates a potential volatility in the perceived importance of issues – any given one might move up or down the agenda as individual circumstances, expectations or concerns change. For example, if global warming is seen as less of a personal threat today than it was in 1997, then general concern about it might have declined too – which, indeed, there is some evidence of happening. (Staggeringly, in the United States the proportion of people who are very or somewhat *satisfied* with 'the state of the nation in terms of protection of the environment' went from 52 per cent in 1993 to 69 per cent in 1999, according to Gallup.[5]) Or, as unemployment continues to decline in Britain, then personal fears about it may do so too, with a consequent decline in its importance as a general issue. Again, there is some evidence that this is, in fact, happening (see Figure 2.2).

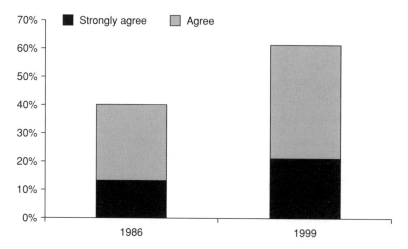

Figure 2.2 Declining sympathy for the unemployed. Proportion who agree that 'there is too much emphasis on the unemployed and they could get jobs if they really wanted to'.

Source: *nVision*, Future Foundation.

Second, social and economic trends point to an increase in concern among consumers along both dimensions. You might have thought that if issues like crime, poverty and educational standards can be addressed and the effects mitigated, then we would experience a decline in those general concerns that are driven by self-focused fears. The reality though is more complex as people's analysis of their own situation is often a relative rather than absolute one. For example, although most people are better-off, income polarization is increasing the downside risks and implications of, for example, failing to keep up in the job market. Although spending on health care and education may be rising (as it has in real terms in the UK) expectations are increasing at an even higher rate, making the delivered service seem inferior. Although we live, in general, in a safer and healthier world, we are more concerned – even paranoid – about a range of issues likely to affect us personally. This is all part of one paradox of a world of 'peace and plenty' that I discuss more fully in Chapters 5 and 8.

And, on the ethical dimension, there is every reason to believe that as more people become better off financially, so they will have the discretion to be concerned about broader issues – to put it crudely, to have the income to be able to afford to be altruistic. Already, as I noted earlier, those in higher income groups and those in professional and managerial occupations are more likely to be concerned about more general, ethical issues. As people move up *Maslow's hierarchy of needs* (see Chapter 5), so they will become more concerned about less material (to them) aspects as well.

These two trends may seem contradictory. While it is true that they apply differentially to different groups in society they are not necessarily in conflict with each other. Consider, for example, a

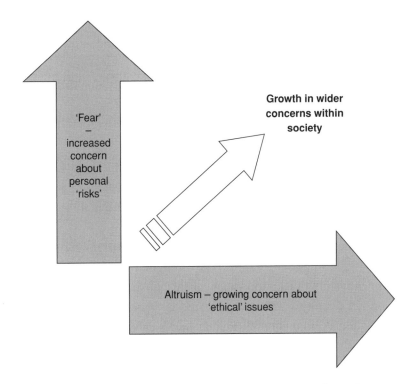

Figure 2.3 The factors driving growing concern. Schematic representation of trends.

Source: adapted from *The Responsible Organisation*, BT/Future Foundation.

middle-class, well-off, middle-aged couple. Irrespective of their political persuasion they may be concerned about the global environment and endangered species and also third world poverty and famine. But, despite their own comfortable situation (with good pensions and insurance as they approach retirement) they may also be concerned about the risks and lack of a safety net that threaten their daughter's job security, their grandchildren's education and the lack of access for all their family to the best possible health care.

So, for both altruistic and not so altruistic reasons, we can expect to see a growth in wider concerns among the population (Figure 2.3). To repeat, the paradox of economic growth and improved social conditions for the majority in the developed world is that it stimulates a growing concern about the perceived wider problems of life.

CITIZENS, CONSUMPTION AND COMPANIES

What evidence is there from consumer research about how this trend might impact on companies? Here, the evidence is not as definitive as it might be, but I still believe some tentative conclusions can be drawn.

First, there is some suggestion in the data that concerns about wider issues might increasingly be influencing consumer choice. I do not want to make too much of this, since it is clear that many consumer decisions are still dominated by basic issues such as price, quality and convenience. (I include under convenience the process of habit-driven purchasing where, to make life easier, people buy the same product week in week out – see Chapter 7.) But, in certain cases these can be overridden by non-functional factors – think for instance of the boycotting of genetically modified foods in Britain in 1999. In other instances, when consumers have to choose between two otherwise identical brands within a given product area, the final decision may be based on specific ethical concerns (whether the cosmetics were tested on animals, for example) or a general perception of the overall ethics of a company.

So, for example, seven out of ten people agree that they would be prepared to pay a little more for products and services from a company if they knew it did a lot for the wider community, with over a quarter agreeing strongly.[6] Now, I accept that questions like these are misleading if taken at face value. They are, after all, easy statements for people to agree with (it costs them nothing after all to answer a market research question). However, it does at least highlight that this is an issue in consumers' minds, even if it does not necessarily prove that it will in reality affect their purchase decisions.

More persuasive are the findings of an exercise that gave more realistic and specific, if still hypothetical, trade-offs to consumers.[7] In four specific products or service situations (a 1.20 kilogram pack of automatic washing powder, a 200 gram jar of instant freeze dried coffee, the weekly grocery shopping and the regular telephone service supplied to the home) the respondents were presented with different formulations for that product or service. This involved not only price, quality and service but also various potential aspects of a company's broader corporate role (environmentally friendly, donates to charity, good employer, helps local community, has a fair trade policy). Unsurprisingly, the results showed how sensitive consumers were to price and quality aspects but it also highlighted that other factors could have an influence too. For washing powder, environmental friendliness was important (in 1997), for coffee it was fair trade (there has been significant campaigning activity in this area including the launch in 1991 of Cafédirect that works in partnership with small-scale coffee producers, guaranteeing fair prices).

When the price differentials were increased in this exercise, these wider issues became less important. This lends not only credibility to the exercise (as people were clearly thinking about the specific formulations being presented to them and making considered opinions on the basis of that) but also reinforces the fact that such concerns are, in effect, 'nice to have' rather than 'must have'.

Another example of how consumer decision making might be influenced in this way is the boycotting of goods or companies. Again, the evidence here is not as clear as might be hoped but certainly a range of questions asked in the 1990s points to an increasing willingness of consumers to pursue such action. Figure 2.4 shows a compilation of survey questions from various sources on the issue of consumer boycotts. Some relate to ethical issues, some to specific environmental ones. Some ask about whether people have at some point engaged in a boycott, others whether they would consider it. As all the questions are slightly different, it is difficult to draw clearcut conclusions but there is certainly an

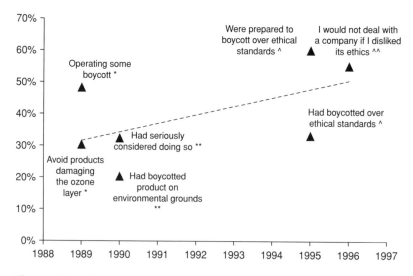

Figure 2.4   A growing readiness to boycott? Percentage agreeing to each statement.

Source: *Who are the Ethical Consumers?*,[8] Co-operative Bank; ★*Daily Telegraph*; ★★Research 2000; ^Gallup; ^^GGT.

indication that the acceptability or desirability of boycotts has increased (a statistically fitted trend line points upwards). This, if you think about it, is not surprising as choice increases (see Chapter 7) and economic discretion grows (see Chapter 5). It is just less costly now for people to boycott a product or brand.

The second main conclusion from consumer research that relates to companies is that people are increasingly cynical about corporate motives and activity. I discuss this again in Chapter 9 and restrict myself here to describing some specific data from consumer studies and how it relates to purchasing activity.

The first set of data on this subject relates to the degree to which consumers trust companies. In a survey[9] respondents were asked how much they trusted specific, named companies on a number of dimensions ranging from being environmentally careful to being honest and truthful in its advertising. Apart from showing huge variations in the degree of overall trust in different companies (with ones like Marks and Spencer, Virgin and Body Shop doing specially well and some, like Nike, Sky and Marlboro, doing particularly badly) it also showed that companies in general are more trusted for some things than others. Companies do best in those areas of basic service delivery like 'providing a good and consistent service', being 'honest and fair in its dealings' and 'treating its customers fairly'. This is to be expected, although arguably the ratings achieved by many companies still leave a lot to be desired. On these three aspects the proportion of people saying they trust the company a great deal or mostly, is around 60 per cent averaged across the companies covered (see Figure 2.5). But should not companies such as these (remember they are all big national and international businesses) be achieving trust levels of 70, 80 or even 90 per cent ? Of the companies in the survey, only Marks and Spencer − with ratings in the 80s in all three areas − consistently reached this sort of level.

But companies do much less well on some of the broader issues that are the focus of this book. So, for example, being good

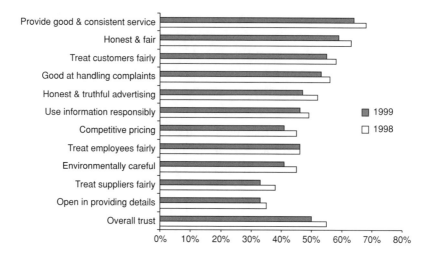

Figure 2.5 Consumers' trust in companies. To what extent do you trust (company) to . . . 'a great deal' or 'mostly'?

Source: Future Foundation/Consumers' Association/Richmond Events.

employers, treating suppliers fairly and being environmentally careful all achieve trust ratings of under 50 per cent. Bottom comes being open in providing details about the company. In fact, as I show later, this is an important component in determining people's overall trust in a brand. Interestingly, being competitive on price also comes fairly low down illustrating, among other things, the continuing price aggressiveness (if I can put it like that) of consumers despite many years of income growth (see Chapter 5).

Two other points come out of this analysis. First, when the research, initially carried out in 1998, was repeated in 1999 we recorded a small decline in trust between the two surveys. In the course of just under a year there had been a minor, but statistically significant, increase in cynicism among consumers. Second, the huge difference between companies on specific aspects of trust is very noticeable.

For example, take two particular, and very important, issues: trusting companies to be 'honest and truthful in their advertising' and to be 'open in providing details about the company'. Figure 2.6 shows that the best companies have twenty times more consumers trusting them (a great deal or mostly) on these aspects than the worst do.

As far as individual companies are concerned, on these dimensions Nike, Sky and Marlboro are towards the bottom of the British

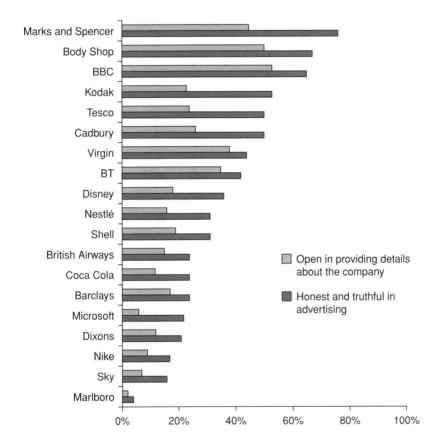

Figure 2.6 Whether company trusted to be 'honest and truthful in advertising'/'open in providing details about the company'. Percentage saying a great deal or mostly.

Source: Future Foundation/Consumers' Association/Richmond Events.

consumers' league. Beyond this, it is noticeable how poorly Microsoft and Coca Cola also fare particularly on being 'open'. British readers may not be surprised to see British Airways, Barclays Bank and high street electrical retailer Dixons not doing so well either.

One reason for looking specifically at these questions on trust revolving around advertising and openness is that a statistical analysis of the data suggests that these two aspects are important ones in determining overall levels of trust in a company, alongside honesty and fairness and consistent service. The conclusion from this study was that trust is built on three core components: honesty, fairness and openness. Another way to describe this last element is the concept of '*transparency*' something that in the new media age is becoming more important.

MAPPING CORPORATE BRANDS

Another exercise using the same piece of research adds further light on the issue of consumer cynicism. It is useful because once again it looks at how specific companies are perceived by consumers. The approach was to ask respondents to choose from a list of 30 adjectives, the six that they most associated with individually named companies. The adjectives ranged from the positive (like honest, trustworthy, innovative) to the not so positive (like cynical, greedy, heartless). People were also asked what six adjectives they would associate with their ideal company.

To try to summarize all these data succinctly a correspondence analysis[10] of the companies and adjectives was carried out. The results are shown in Figure 2.7 and are based on all consumers' views of companies whether they use them or not. Interestingly, the results are almost identical when restricted to regular users of the company suggesting that these perceptions are broadly based,

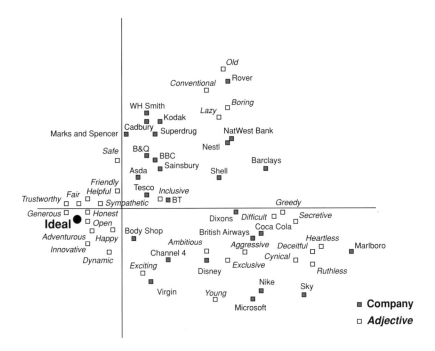

Figure 2.7 Mapping brands and adjectives. Analysis of adjectives associated with certain brands.

Source: Future Foundation/Consumers' Association/Richmond Events.

robust and represent real feelings about the businesses in question.

If you look at the 'map' you can see, in effect, two dimensions. One is an old/conventional versus dynamic/innovative axis (top to bottom), the other a sympathetic/trustworthy versus ruthless/greedy one (left to right).

On this basis, what people want in their ideal company is a sympathetic organization they can trust but also one that is dynamic and innovative. None of the companies in the survey achieved this. The companies that did best were, to a greater or lesser degree, either conventional, safe and sympathetic (like Marks and Spencer, Cadbury and Kodak) or exciting, innovative and dynamic (like Virgin and Body Shop). The direct comparisons are interesting:

Body Shop is seen as more sympathetic than Virgin but less dynamic; Tesco is seen as more dynamic than Sainsbury but less trustworthy.

What is perhaps most interesting are the companies occupying the area in the bottom right-hand corner of the map. The adjectives respondents associated with these companies are not ideal brand attributes: ruthless, deceitful, greedy, cynical and the like. Some of the world's biggest brands are here – Marlboro, Nike, Coca Cola and Microsoft – as is British satellite broadcaster Sky. To reinforce the point, listed in Table 2.1 are the top five adjectives that were associated with three of the world's best-known brands. They are set alongside the adjectives for Virgin, a brand that if not as 'famous' still has significant global brand awareness and certainly was better placed on the map. The contrast is stark.

However, many of these poorly ranked brands (in terms of adjectives) have been highly successful in commercial terms over the last few years. On one measure of this, seven of the companies included in the survey rank within Interbrand's top 60 world brands by brand value.[11] But Figure 2.8 shows how many of these fall in the 'nether' zone of the adjectives map.

This raises some important questions. If these companies have such a strong brand valuation and if some are highly successful commercially, why do they have such negative associations in some customers' minds? More importantly, does it therefore matter whether consumers think you are greedy or ruthless or cynical if they keep buying your products?

I believe it does for the simple reason that past or current commercial success is no guarantee of success in the future. Moreover, the chances of a company or brand failing in the future depend in part on current perceptions of it. In any case, some of these companies have been successful in part because of the market conditions under which they operate. An obvious example from those businesses included in this survey is British satellite broadcaster Sky.

Table 2.1 Adjectives associated with certain companies

Marlboro	%	Nike	%	Coca Cola	%	Virgin	%
Cynical	68	Ambitious	48	Aggressive	44	Innovative	60
Ruthless	59	Aggressive	44	Ambitious	44	Dynamic	51
Heartless	58	Greedy	39	Greedy	39	Ambitious	50
Secretive	58	Exclusive	33	Secretive	35	Adventurous	46
Deceitful	54	Cynical	31	Ruthless	33	Exciting	40

Souce: Future Foundation/Consumers' Association/Richmond Events.

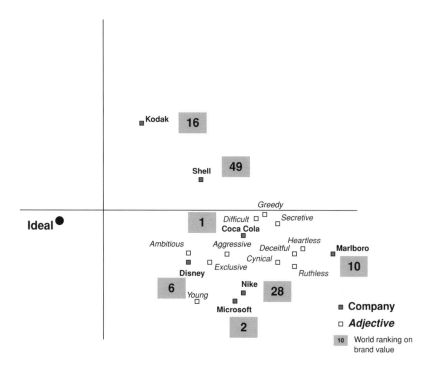

Figure 2.8 Brand value – do we have the right measures? Brand and adjective 'map' and ranking on Interbrand's brand value.

Source: Interbrand, Future Foundation/Consumers' Association/Richmond Events.

Thanks to a benign regulatory environment Sky has, until now, been the only satellite broadcaster in Britain. Of course it does have multi-channel competitors in the form of cable companies, but cable is still being rolled out across the country. Sky also now has a terrestrial digital television competitor in ONdigital but for many years benefited from first mover advantage. Through its own skill and audacity, Sky also bought film and sports rights giving it a huge advantage in content too. (Again, these are available through the cable operators but are heavily branded as Sky and the revenues, of course, go to Sky.) Thus, many people had little option but to subscribe to the Sky service, either directly or through cable operators. The same continues to happen with Sky's new digital offer.

Consider some of the other companies in that quadrant of the map. Microsoft too is in a near monopoly position with its Windows products and although Coca Cola has a major competitor in Pepsi Cola, between them they account for the vast majority of cola sales around the world. Marlboro, although it has many competitors, sells an addictive product that has no alternative – the market may not be a monopoly but the product certainly is.

Indeed, the only brand in that quadrant of the map that stands out as not having some special market factors in its favour is Nike. The poor perception of Nike is almost certainly linked to the bad publicity it has received over the claimed ill-treatment of its workers in its third world factories (see Chapter 9). To date, that does not seem to have affected its commercial success but whether that will still be the case in the future remains to be seen.

What is clearly true is that if any of these companies were asked whether they were happy to have themselves perceived in this way, the answer would be a resounding no. This is not an ideal positioning to have and most businesses in this situation, whatever their current commercial fortunes, would seek to address it. Some already have.

Sky, perhaps in part because it is starting to face real competition for the first time, has tried to rid itself of its old aggressive, 'macho' image. Mark Booth, CEO from 1997 until 1999 made a start in June 1998 when he said 'BSkyB has been aggressive with its pricing in the past, and there is a trust issue we are committed to turning round'.[12] Recent indications from the company suggest that the initiative is being maintained.

Coca Cola too has had a change of heart – this, though, prompted by a poor set of results. As new Chairman and Chief Executive Douglas Daft baldly put it: 'After 15 years of consistent success, [in 1999] we endured a year of dramatic setbacks'.[13] Daft's response has been to develop a new strategy that tries to reconnect the company with society. This is built around three strands:

1. 'Think local, act local' – the aim here being to reconnect to the local communities where, after all, local people drink individual bottles in local settings.
2. 'Focus as a pure marketing company' – since, as Daft notes, Coca Cola's 'success flows from the strength of our brands, and our ability to relate to people'.
3. 'Lead as model citizens' – because 'in every community where we sell our brands, we must remember we do not do business in markets; we do business in societies.'[14]

It is clear that Douglas Daft recognizes that the way Coca Cola is perceived across the globe leaves much to be desired – and, more importantly, that it is unsustainable. In his mind, although he has not put it exactly in this way, it needs to have a better understanding of, and relationship with, society – to be, in other words, a citizen brand.

All this suggests that many large, multinational companies not only recognize that there are negative feelings about them but also recognize they should do something about it. Whether they are doing enough is another matter.

THE IMPACT ON CONSUMERS

If we take two of the key points from this chapter and think of their combined impact, then the potential effect on companies is profound.

First, I have shown that as affluence increases consumers become more likely to change their purchasing patterns as a result of wider concerns – they are more likely to be 'ethical' consumers. Second, people are becoming increasingly cynical of companies' behaviour. Taken together, this suggests that the public's perception of a corporation's attitude to and understanding of broader social issues and, indeed, that company's behaviour in society at large, is becoming more influential in determining buying patterns and brand choice.

Analysis of consumer survey data covering the last twenty years certainly seems to support this thesis. The surveys initially conducted by market research company Taylor Nelson (now Taylor Nelson Sofres) and now continued by the Future Foundation investigate a range of social values and consumer attitudes.[15] I have re-analysed some of the questions to consider these two aspects of 'ethical' consumption and cynicism towards companies. For the first dimension – how wider concerns might be influencing consumer behaviour – I created an index by combining each respondent's responses to two questions:[16]

■ how people felt about 'companies that do things which are profitable but not morally right' (and, in particular, whether it made them angry);

■ agreement with the statement: 'I would be willing to pay as much as 10 per cent more a week for grocery items if I could be sure that they would not harm the environment'.

To assess the question of cynicism towards companies I used agreement (and disagreement) with the statement:

■ 'most companies in this country are fair to consumers'.

As before in this chapter, these questions are far from ideal. If we were seeking to specifically research these issues today we would ask different and more direct questions. But, these questions do allow us to get a feel for the issues under consideration and do at least allow us to compare change in consumer attitudes over a long period of time.

Specifically, I wanted to assess whether the proportion of consumers who were potentially influenced by wider or 'ethical' concerns *and* were cynical about company behaviour had increased. These, after all, are those consumers most likely to be aware of, and interested in, citizen brands. Two definitions were used. A stricter one required respondents to have a score of eight or more out of ten on the 'ethical' index and to have actively disagreed that companies are fair to consumers. A less restrictive definition was based on a score of seven or more on the index (in other words, a strong or reasonable strength of feeling on at least one of the questions) and a lack of agreement (as opposed to active disagreement) that companies are fair.[17] The results, as set out in Figure 2.9, make interesting reading.

Three main points can be drawn from this analysis. First, the proportion of the population likely to be influenced by a business's wider actions and roles in society (and therefore likely to support the citizen brand concept) has increased. Second, the

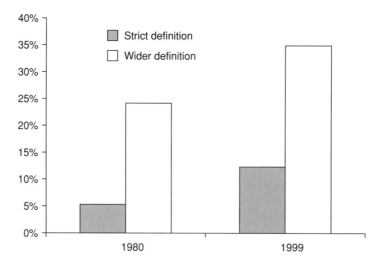

Figure 2.9 Seeking citizen brands? Proportion of consumers who are potentially influenced by wider/'ethical' issues *and* who are cynical about companies – defined in two ways.

Source: *n*Vision, Future Foundation.

proportion of 'hard nuts' – those with the most strongly held ethical and anti-corporatist views – is much smaller than those with a still concerned but more equivocal outlook. This is consistent with other research studies in the area of ethical consumption. Third, it still affects only a minority of the consuming public.

This last point is an important one since at this rate it might take perhaps 20 years before the majority of the population could be characterized as caring about citizen brands. It would, however, be a mistake in my view to interpret it like this. For a start, few companies can ignore even 15 per cent of their consumers let alone 35 per cent. Then, there is the fact that, as I showed earlier, those consumers who many companies most cherish – those in higher social grades and with most discretionary spending power – are more likely to have these wider concerns and, research shows, more likely to pay a price premium for products embracing them. Then there are the dynamics within society. As the nature of work changes, so more people are entering managerial, professional and administrative occupations – moving into higher social grades. Society is ageing too and, as I show in Chapter 9, it is the 'new' old – those who are passing their 50th birthday now or during the next 10 years – who are the most cynical about companies. Finally, it is clear that attitudes towards companies, their operating practices and their relationship with society has suddenly become a hot and potentially disruptive issue as I discuss also in Chapter 9. Whether this is just a flash in the pan remains to be seen. I suspect it is not, but in any case, surely it would be foolish for the business world to dismiss it as such.

THE RELATIONSHIP BETWEEN LOYALTY, TRUST AND CORPORATE CITIZENSHIP

The final piece of analysis of consumer research that I wish to draw on involves using multivariate statistical techniques to look at the relationship between some of the issues I have considered in this chapter. In particular, I want to investigate how perceptions of a company relate to actual consumer behaviour (or at least the behaviour claimed in the survey). The survey,[18] provides a unique opportunity to do this because it asks about people's views on specific named companies on a range of dimensions as well as their usage of those companies and their products. Thus, questions were asked not only about different aspects of trust (as shown in Figure 2.5) but also about: satisfaction with the company; whether it was viewed as a good corporate citizen;[19] whether it was seen as open and accessible; and whether its advertising and press coverage had been good over the past year. The companies asked about were those listed in Figure 2.6.

From the analysis, a picture emerges of the processes by which some of these factors are linked. We cannot prove that these are causal relationships – that, for example, increasing consumers' access to a company will lead inevitably to an increase in trust – but we can, in my view, develop a plausible model that implies causality. It goes like this.

■ Not surprisingly, the most important factor determining customer loyalty is customer satisfaction. A consumer who is satisfied with a company and its services is more likely to continue to buy its products. Or, more importantly, and to put it the other way, consumers who are dissatisfied are likely to change to different suppliers. This is not only an intuitively obvious point but has been proven in numerous studies. Its significance here is in emphasizing the importance to commercial success of the basic aspects of any offer – providing good quality products and services, offering competitive prices and ensuring a good purchasing experience and after-sales service. This will obviously continue to be the case in the future.

■ But the analysis also showed that trusting a company is important to loyalty too. Satisfaction with a company and trust in it are closely correlated. So, in part, you trust a company because it provides a satisfactory service. In this sense, a measure of trust and a measure of satisfaction are, in fact, measuring the same thing.[20] But, the statistical analysis shows that they are not exactly the same thing – that there is something else about trust that has the effect of increasing customer loyalty. So, for example, some respondents were loyal to a company despite relatively low satisfaction because, as far as we can tell from this survey, they trusted it. Overall then, satisfaction is the main factor determining brand loyalty with trust having a separate and secondary impact too.

■ Beyond providing a satisfactory service what else causes people to trust a company? Here the results of the analysis get interesting. Of the factors covered in the survey the most important determinant of trust is whether the company is seen to be a good corporate citizen. The second is whether it is seen as being open and accessible to consumers (for information or complaints, for example) – a 'transparent' organization as I described it earlier. Again, these two factors are in themselves related: people are more likely to think a company is a good corporate citizen if they believe it is a transparent organization and vice versa.

■ The other, albeit much weaker, aspect that appears to be associated with higher trust (and hence increased loyalty) is communications activity. Interestingly, good press coverage appears to be more important than good advertising. Figure 2.10 illustrates this by plotting for each company in the survey the proportion of respondents saying they trusted the company a great deal or mostly against the proportion saying they felt the company had received very or fairly good press coverage in the last year. This is the left-hand diagram in the figure. The right-hand diagram does the same exercise but plots trust against whether the company was felt to have produced excellent or very good advertising. In each diagram a line of best fit is

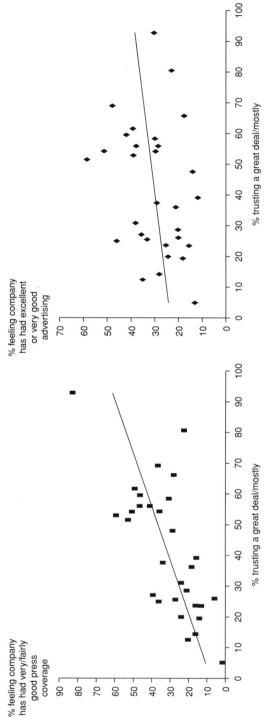

Figure 2.10 The relationship between communications activity and trust. Does press activity have more of an impact?

Source: Future Foundation/Consumers' Association/Richmond Events.

included to show the direction of the relationship between the variables. It can be seen that the line for press coverage is much steeper than that for advertising – good press coverage appears to be more strongly related to trust than good advertising does.

To summarize this, Figure 2.11 provides a simplified repre-sentation of the relationships, together with my interpretation of how the process works. The main factor driving customer loyalty is satisfaction with the company, product or service. Satisfaction tends to lead to increased trust in the company or brand, but trust in its own right, and independently, makes the customer more loyal. As well as satisfaction helping to increase trust, so do some general perceptions about the company and specifically whether

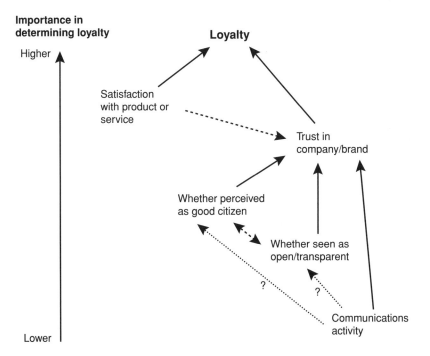

Figure 2.11 A model of citizenship and loyalty. Schematic represen-tation of the process.

Source: Future Foundation.

it is felt to be a good corporate citizen and to be open and accessible to consumers. Again, although these two factors are related – a perception of being accessible is likely to enhance the belief that the organization is a good citizen – they also have their separate impact on trust. This implies that to maximize trust a business needs to be both a responsible citizen and a transparent organization. Finally, good communications activity can increase trust too. The full process by which this works cannot be deduced from this particular survey, but at least part of the explanation is surely that good communications help to generate a perception of citizenship and transparency.

BRANDS, CITIZENSHIP AND CONSUMERS

So, what have we learned from this chapter and its analysis of a range of consumer surveys?

First, that people's concerns about wider issues are the result of both personal fears and more altruistic feelings. This is neither new nor contentious. But the potential implications are. For a start, the strength of feeling about specific concerns and the level of support for specific ethical issues could well become increasingly volatile. This will make it harder for companies to keep up with the consuming public's agenda. At the same time, I have argued that the overall range and extent of such concerns will grow over time.

Second, is that consumers' concerns about wider issues are increasingly impacting on their perceptions of companies and their purchasing decisions. This is important because it is happening at a time when consumers are becoming more cynical about companies themselves. The effect is an increasing number of consumers who are not only sceptical about companies' aims and actions but are also happy to boycott their products.

Third, and related to this, the adjectives some consumers most associate with some companies are, to say the least, far from ideal as far as those companies, presumably, are concerned. Some of the world's biggest brands may be ubiquitous, 'famous', have great brand recall and be commercially successful but underneath that there are some negative connotations in consumers' minds. This suggests that current measures of brand 'value' may be missing something. Certainly, some brands should be feeling rather uneasy.

Finally, the importance of trust – and through that, of citizenship and transparency – on customer loyalty has been demonstrated. So, being a good corporate citizen (and being open and accessible is surely, in itself, a component of that) is already important for corporate and brand success. For a variety of reasons that I discuss later it seems likely that it will become more so in the future.

These are all important points and I pick up and develop a number of them in later chapters. I also consider the implications for business strategy and behaviour. But first, I want to consider some of the philosophical objections to corporate citizenship and do that by looking at the historical development of it.

BEYOND
PHILANTHROPY

BEYOND PHILANTHROPY

Searching for a New Consensus

*D*espite all the evidence that good corporate citizens are more commercially successful, there continues to be a vigorous argument about the roles and responsibilities of companies. On the one side are those who believe that a company's main (and sometimes sole) responsibility is to its owners/shareholders. On the other are people who argue that companies have a moral and ethical responsibility to consider a wider range of stakeholders.

At one level, the existence of this debate seems strange. You would have thought that given the evidence from the previous two chapters shareholders would be clamouring for companies to be better corporate citizens. They would actively want the companies they invest in to have a better awareness and understanding of society's concerns, sometimes even taking a more active role in directly helping to address social and economic problems. They would want a company to be open and transparent and to be great employers. They should, according to the survey quoted in Chapter 1, take a strong view about excessive executive pay.

And you would have thought that managers, wishing to maximize shareholder returns, would want to follow these strategies too (including keeping their own remuneration within reasonable bounds).

Yet on the whole shareholders and business managers do not think or act like this. In part, this reflects the overly short-term focus that seems to dominate Anglo-American capitalism in particular. But this cannot be the whole story and it remains surprising that supposedly pragmatic business managers ignore the overwhelming evidence on the relationship between corporate citizenship and commercial performance.

Part of the problem, it seems to me, is a corporate culture rooted in the 1980s and 1990s (which in itself was a reaction to previous times) that fails to appreciate the changes in the social, economic and cultural environment. Part is the result of ideological positioning within a debate that I believe is, in fact, sterile and meaningless. And, part is an understandable reluctance to accept an idea that is less than fully understood – why should corporate citizenship initiatives be a profitable use of a company's resources? The first two points are discussed in this chapter, the last in the next one.

FORWARD TO THE PAST

At least since the advent of industrialization (and probably even before then) some business leaders have taken a philanthropic view of their responsibilities to society. In Victorian Britain, awareness of the terrible living conditions that many people experienced, particularly in urban areas, led employers like Joseph Rowntree and George Cadbury to take positive steps to address the problems. In many ways this was driven by their religious convictions.

With the onset of industrialisation in Britain . . . the Puritan ethic was one of the major ideological alternatives available to aspiring and successful industrialists. Though diluted by the economics of Adam Smith, the secular self-help notions of Samuel Smiles, and the social Darwinism of Herbert Spencer, the Calvinist code morally and spiritually energised English capitalism through the decades of Victorian prosperity.[1]

George Cadbury felt he had a duty 'to seek continuously to improve the material conditions of men'.[2] His construction of a new 'village' for his workers at Bourneville was in part his contribution to solving the wider housing problems of the working class created by industrialization.

Though Cadbury and Rowntree are probably the best known for the provisions they made for their employees, other manufacturers preceded them. For example Titus Salt – in building 800 model dwellings – was 'the first great British manufacturer to recognise that the requirements of [his] employees should be the first charge on the profits from the firm'.[3] The creation of Saltaire went on to include the building of a Congregational church, factory schools, baths, a public wash house, alms houses, an infirmary and a club house . . . and the presentation to the inhabitants of a park.

The main motivations for these philanthropic attitudes were not dissimilar to, and perhaps in part inherited from, those of the landed gentry in the agricultural economy:

■ a moral or ethical view on social justice (often built around religious convictions),
■ and a paternalistic approach to workers' needs and rights.

For example, William Lever regarded his building of Port Sunlight as a form of profit sharing, but with a firmly paternalistic tone to it. He said:

Frankly, £8 is soon spent, and will not do you much good if you send it down your throats in the form of bottles of whisky, bags of sweets, or fat geese for Christmas. On the other hand, if you leave this money with me, I shall provide for you everything that makes life pleasant – viz, nice houses, comfortable homes and healthy recreation. Besides I am disposed to allow profit sharing in no other form.[4]

In America, similar, but slightly more pragmatic, attitudes were being espoused by the likes of Henry Ford:

I don't believe we should make such an awful profit on our cars. A reasonable profit is right, but not too much. I hold that it is better to sell a large number of cars at a reasonably small profit . . . I hold this because it enables a larger number of people to buy and enjoy the use of a car and because it gives a larger number of men employment at good wages. Those are the two aims I have in life.[5]

Ford was responding to criticism over his high wage rates (roughly double the industry standard) and aggressive pricing policies that had seen a more than 50 per cent reduction in prices between 1908 and 1916, even though demand for his cars exceeded supply. Although now, we might view this as pragmatic business decision-making, at the time it caused a furore in the business world. The *Wall Street Journal* claimed Ford had a 'naïve wish for social improvement' and had injected 'spiritual principles into a field where they do not belong', while two shareholders took legal action against him to stop such 'philanthropic' activity.[6]

THE END OF PHILANTHROPY?

As the twentieth century progressed though, the state became more involved in welfare provision, the regulation of corporate behaviour and the conditions under which people worked. Across Europe, welfare state systems were initiated, most notably in Britain in 1946. At the same time, many industries were brought under state control.

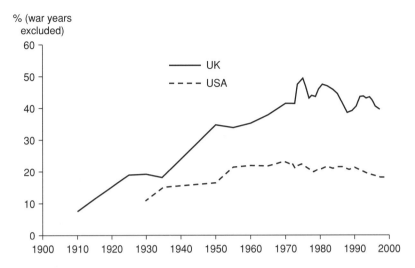

Figure 3.1 Government spending as a proportion of GDP.

Source: Office of National Statistics, Bureau of Economic Analysis (US Department of Commerce).

The involvement of the state hit a peak in the UK in the mid-1970s when government spending reached nearly 50 per cent of Gross Domestic Product. A similar, but less extreme pattern occurred in the United States too, with the total of federal and state spending peaking, at a bit under 25 per cent, also in the 1970s (Figure 3.1).

The rise in state involvement in welfare is illustrated by the legislation that was enacted during the course of the industrialization process. In Britain in the hundred year period between the middle of the nineteenth and twentieth centuries, a whole host of welfare related acts of parliament were passed, ranging from those covering poverty, to health, to workers' rights. The immediate post-war era represented the height of this activity, with the Labour government's launch of the National Health Service (and, widespread nationalization).

A look at the legislation during this period suggests three distinct phases (see Figure 3.2). First, to counter the worst problems of the industrial revolution were initiatives to alleviate the basic problems of acute poverty and public health issues – what might be called *the social protection era.* As workers began to organize themselves better (and as the ideologies of Marxism and Socialism developed), the legislative programme moved towards aspects of *mutuality and representation.* In the twentieth century the focus changed to more universal benefits and rights: pensions, education and health care. Taken with the privatization of key industries and

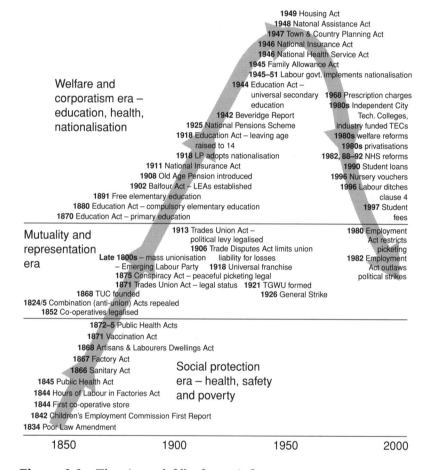

Welfare and corporatism era – education, health, nationalisation

1949 Housing Act
1948 Natonal Assistance Act
1947 Town & Country Planning Act
1946 National Insurance Act
1946 National Health Service Act
1945 Family Allowance Act
1945–51 Labour govt. implements nationalisation
1944 Education Act – universal secondary education
1942 Beveridge Report
1925 National Pensions Scheme
1918 Education Act – leaving age raised to 14
1918 LP adopts nationalisation
1911 National Insurance Act
1908 Old Age Pension introduced
1902 Balfour Act – LEAs established
1891 Free elementary education
1880 Education Act – compulsory elementary education
1870 Education Act – primary education

1968 Prescription charges
1980s Independent City Tech. Colleges, industry funded TECs
1980s welfare reforms
1980s privatisations
1982, 88–92 NHS reforms
1990 Student loans
1996 Nursery vouchers
1996 Labour ditches clause 4
1997 Student fees

Mutuality and representation era

1913 Trades Union Act – political levy legalised
1906 Trade Disputes Act limits union liability for losses
Late 1800s – mass unionisation
– Emerging Labour Party **1918** Universal franchise
1875 Conspiracy Act – peaceful picketing legal
1871 Trades Union Act – legal status **1921** TGWU formed
1868 TUC founded
1824/5 Combination (anti-union) Acts repealed
1852 Co-operatives legalised
1926 General Strike

1980 Employment Act restricts picketing
1982 Employment Act outlaws political strikes

1872–5 Public Health Acts
1871 Vaccination Act
1868 Artisans & Labourers Dwellings Act
1867 Factory Act
1866 Sanitary Act
1845 Public Health Act
1844 Hours of Labour in Factories Act
1844 First co-operative store
1842 Children's Employment Commission First Report
1834 Poor Law Amendment

Social protection era – health, safety and poverty

| 1850 | 1900 | 1950 | 2000 |

Figure 3.2 The rise and fall of state influence.

Source: *The Responsible Organisation,* BT/Future Foundation.

the centralized organization of many public services this could be labelled as the *corporatist welfare era*.

By the 1970s, however, the welfare state was coming under increasing strain and criticism. From that point on, the legislative programme changed – away from universal benefits and towards targeted benefits, means testing and payment for certain items or activities (for example, prescription charges – introduced, perhaps ironically, by a Labour government). It is perhaps no surprise that government spending started to fall at this time and the fact that this has been experienced in other countries suggests the change in mood was not restricted to Britain.

It is my contention that the development of the welfare state, universal benefits and adequate 'safety nets' had a profound influence on the way business and others viewed its role in society.

If the state was ensuring that citizens and workers would be provided for in moments of need, then why did companies need to be philanthropic? If a reasonable safety net existed for those, say, without work (although in the 1950s and 1960s there was effectively full employment in Britain), then why would employees care about or expect employers to provide philanthropy? Equally, having secured a whole range of rights as workers – and, alongside that, become less deferential to their bosses – why should people want or accept paternalist hand-outs or moralistic exhortations from corporations?

The *enlightened self-interest* that was a key factor in the paternalistic, philanthropy of the earlier industrialists (see below) was no longer relevant. Philanthropy was neither needed nor wanted. The only reason why companies might engage in socially responsible behaviour was therefore for purely ethical reasons. But this too, was under threat.

In Britain, Margaret Thatcher was elected in 1979 on a platform which, among other things, set out to reduce the influence of the state on people's lives. Ronald Reagan closely followed her in the United States and later, and to varying degrees, so did most other developed countries. The privatization of previously publicly owned corporations, for example, continues unabated across the world.

If the culture of the state was in decline, the result appeared to be the ascendancy of the cult of business. Business, once a dirty word in many social democracies, was now lauded (and continues to be so) by politicians. Capitalism and the law of the market were seen as the correct way to run economies. Profits were 'cool' and by the end of the 1980s even 'greed was good' (according to Gordon Gekko).[7] All this was reinforced when European communism collapsed in 1989. It was, so some argued, 'the end of history'.[8] Capitalism had won.

The impact on corporate citizenship was interesting. Because business was now seen as the saviour of all things, it was encouraged to get involved in 'social' activity. But in reality, business itself was concentrating on the bottom line. As one business leader admitted in an interview with the Future Foundation:

> Businesses were definitely expected to do more in the Thatcher years, plus in a general sense business success was seen as the answer to everything. But a lot of corporate social activity in the 80s was a sham.[9]

But, by the early 1990s, as recession swept the world some started to question the impact of unrestrained capitalism and the cult of shareholder value. As income polarization increased in many countries (see Figure 3.3), politicians and business people alike began to ponder the implications. One result was the development of a new political philosophy, as personified by Bill Clinton and Tony Blair, which emphasized the twin goals of entrepreneurial, market economies and social justice. Another, was the anti-capitalist, anti-multinational movement as typified by the writings of Naomi Klein[10] and George Monbiot.[11]

Business people were starting to worry too. John Banham, then director general of the Confederation of British Industry,

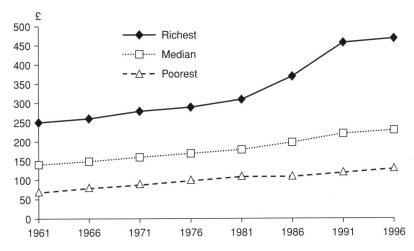

Figure 3.3 Increasing income polarization. Weekly income before housing costs by income group (UK).

Source: *The Acheson Report*, 1998.

emphasized in 1991 the need for corporate involvement in helping with social and economic problems:

> It is a chilling prospect, as any visitor to the South Bronx or parts of Lambeth will confirm. An increasingly affluent majority will live uneasily alongside an increasingly deprived, resentful and repressed minority, who will not be able to use the ballot box to secure a redistribution of wealth to their advantage.[12]

The fear was, and remains, that if the prosperity and cohesiveness of society were threatened, then business itself would suffer. As Andrew Wilson of Ashridge Management College noted in 1995: 'Today, there is growing acceptance of the view that if business is to prosper, the environment in which it operates must prosper, too'.[13]

THE END OF THE ARGUMENT?

This is the context in which the current debate about corporate citizenship takes place and I think it helps to explain the nature of the heated dispute about the role of the company in society. I believe it also offers the prospect of conciliation between the opposing points of view.

On the one hand there are those who believe that there is a whole range of social and economic problems in the world that need addressing. Given the triumph of market capitalism and the increasingly dominant role of business in both national and global economies, and given the reduction in the scope and scale of what the state can do, business has a responsibility, an obligation, to do more. In the context of growing income polarization, and particularly the excessive, 'fat cat' pay of senior executives (particularly in the Anglo-Saxon economies – see Figure 3.4), this is seen as nothing less than a moral obligation.

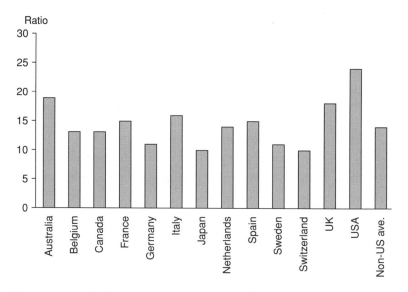

Figure 3.4 Chief Executive Officer pay in advanced countries. Ratio of CEO to worker pay.

Source: *The State of Working America*, 1999.

A recent example of this sentiment is contained in Will Hutton's pamphlet *Society Bites Back*:[14]

> It is a *moral obligation*. The new centrality of business in contemporary life means that business must acknowledge that it too has citizenship responsibilities. Victory in the ideological battle means that paradoxically it has never had greater *obligations* to act with integrity and wider social purpose. [My emphasis]

On the other side of the argument are those who believe that those running businesses have one main responsibility – to maximize shareholder value. They do not believe it is the role of business to get involved in other activities, as famously summarized by Milton Friedman's comment that 'a corporation's social responsibility is to make a profit'.

Proponents of this view, worry that attention to corporate citizenship issues will divert business managers from their main responsibilities. *Financial Times* journalist Samuel Brittan echoed this fear in 1996:[15]

> Everyone is supposed to promote the interests of everyone else and no-one is really accountable for anything. Management is theoretically responsible not only to shareholders or even to workers, but to suppliers, customers and the public at large. This has no operational meaning. In practice it is simply a charter for management to do what it likes without accountability to the owners of the business.

The debate between the two sides has become increasingly heated and, it seems to me, pedantic. An exchange of letters in the *Financial Times* in the summer of 1999 makes the point. Samuel Brittan (who had noticeably softened his stance since his 1996 piece) had written an article with the sub-heading: 'An independent committee is trying to find a route through the minefield of rival ideas about the duties of directors'.[16] In it he discussed whether directors should be *permitted* or *required* to take account of the interests of non-shareholders and the distinction between who and what directors took into account when making their decision and who they were responsible for. It drew a smart response from Alastair Ross Goobey, chief executive of Hermes Pensions Management:

> Sir Samuel Brittan . . . quotes Jonathan Charkham on the distinction between 'taking account' and being 'responsible to'; an encapsulation of this, agreed by Lord Haskins and Mark Goyder of the Centre for Tomorrow's Company, leading 'stakeholder' advocates, is that a company's board is responsible *for* its relationships with employees, customers, suppliers, the environment and society, but it is responsible *to* its shareholders.[17]

Mark Goyder replied:

> Directors are accountable to shareholders. They owe their duty to the company. They are bound to have regard to the interests of shareholders, but that obligation is not confined to the current body of shareholders. That is a matter of law now, although too few directors and too few of their legal advisers understand it. Too many seem to imagine that they are doing their duty if they serve the interests of current shareholders at the expense of the future well-being of the company.[18]

This is what the debate had come down to: the prepositions 'to' and 'for'. Who a company is responsible *to* and who is it responsible *for*. And, as Mark Goyder points out, whether the responsibility is to/for current or future generations.

In fact, I believe behind this there is a growing consensus of sorts. On the one hand, many business people recognize that there are problems (as I noted earlier) and that it is in their own interests as citizens and business managers for companies to be more 'engaged' in society. On the other hand, an increasing number of those on the other side of the debate are recognizing that the profit motive is a legitimate and primary concern of business. John Elkington and others, for example, have emphasized the importance of profits while campaigning for improved social and environmental awareness and activity – often referred to as the 'double' or 'triple bottom-line' approach.[19]

The narrowing gap between the two sides suggests that a subtle shift in the analysis and position of each side could lead to agreement. This requires two things. First, as I argued in the introduction to this book, it would be better to view corporate citizenship not as an *obligation* but as something of *mutual benefit* arising out of the interdependent *relationship* between business and society. Second, companies need to get away from an overly short-term focus and be bolder in promoting good citizenship as being in shareholders' longer-term interests.

This suggests that those campaigning for business to be more 'engaged' with society might do better not to suggest that this is a moral, ethical or philanthropic issue and should certainly avoid sounding righteous or political. Business activity in this area is not a substitute for the state. Rather, it is about getting business to engage in citizenship because it is good for society and good for business. Realistically, we must recognize the pressures on companies in today's global economy and their justifiable need to make profits. The focus therefore needs to be on the business case for any initiative, emphasizing that decisions about citizenship are legitimate business decisions. It is important to make clear that this is not, as Samuel Brittan feared, 'a charter for management to do what it likes without accountability' but rather a pragmatic analysis for the benefit of shareholders.

Those on the shareholder-is-supreme side of the argument should see this as a straightforward business issue. They might do better to forgo pedantic debates about who responsibilities are to or for and just get on with making the correct strategic choices. Here, the evidence is overwhelming. In the long run, being a good corporate citizen is a sensible strategy because:

- As I have shown in the past two chapters, it is correlated to commercial success.
- It is just plain good business sense. Management gurus implore companies to be great employers – this is accepted as a

perfectly sensible strategy. They exhort the need to put the customer at the centre of the company and this is embraced without question. Citizenship – a company's relationship with society and the people (including customers and employees) and organizations within it – is just another aspect of this.

■ As I argue throughout this book citizenship is important because increasingly it impacts on corporate and product branding. If corporate citizenship is an integral part of branding, and branding is a major responsibility of the marketing function, and marketing is recognized as an increasingly important strategic issue, is not corporate citizenship a strategic issue?

Crucially then, this is not about benefaction or philanthropy. Importantly, as the business case becomes increasingly accepted, being a citizen brand will not be seen as a 'nice-to-have' add-on but as a crucial aspect of corporate strategy. Indeed, I suspect that the nature of the criticism that corporate managers worry about will change. At present, I get the feeling that a number of executives fear castigation for wasting time and resources on 'fluffy' citizenship activities rather than concentrating on hard-nosed business problems and shareholders' needs. In the future their concern is more likely to be the charge that they are jeopardizing shareholder needs by ignoring such citizenship issues.

BACK TO THE FUTURE?

Some might dismiss my arguments as nothing new. It sounds very similar to the 'enlightened self interest' that Robert W. Johnson Jr, of Johnson & Johnson, referred to as long ago as 1935:

> In 1935 Johnson . . . echoed these sentiments in a philosophy that he called 'enlightened self-interest' wherein '*service to customers* [his emphasis] comes first . . . service to employees and management second, and . . . service to stockholders last'. Later (in 1943), he added service to the

community to the list (still ahead of service to shareholders) . . . 'When these things have been done,' he wrote, 'the stockholders should receive a fair return.' Although J&J has periodically reviewed and lightly revised the wording of the credo since 1943, the essential ideology – the hierarchy of responsibilities descending from customers down to shareholders and the explicit emphasis on fair return rather thanmaximum return – has remained consistent throughout.[20]

Similar though this might sound, there are in fact some important differences. First, of course, is that Johnson & Johnson was fairly unique in those days. There were other companies that held similar views, Ford who I mentioned earlier being one. But most companies did not follow and have not followed this credo. Nowadays though, this sort of ethos should, in principle if not yet in reality, resonate with a much wider range of companies.

Second, the tone is one of ethical obligation that has to be balanced against profitability (or level of return as Robert W. Johnson Jr put it). Shareholders can only have a 'fair return' rather than a 'maximum return' because of responsibilities to others. The way I would rewrite this in the current climate would be to talk about managing relationships with relevant parties (rather than responsibilities) in order to maximize returns. I would also stress Mark Goyder's point that the company's managers need to manage not only for today but for tomorrow too. (Of course, there will always be businesses that are run in an exploitative manner to maximize the short-term rewards for their shareholders and executives, but this book is not intended for such companies or their managers.)

Some readers may feel I am making a semantic point. Is there much difference between being a good corporate citizen because you believe in it and because shareholders will benefit from it (the Johnson approach) and my alternative that to maximize shareholder returns you need to be a good corporate citizen? At one level, I suspect not – the outcome is much the same in terms of what any individual company might actually do in its corporate citizenship activity. But, I would argue that my formulation will be more attractive to a broader range of companies as it retains the primary importance of shareholders and long-term profitability. In that way it would have a bigger impact on society at large, ironically better meeting the demands of corporate responsibility campaigners themselves.

So, in the first two chapters of this book I have provided real, and I hope persuasive, evidence that being a citizen brand is a commercially sound strategy. In this chapter I have addressed the political and philosophical arguments against being a citizen brand. But one philosophical barrier remains. It might work, it might be politically OK but *why* does it work? Until that can be explained persuasively there is the danger that some may remain unconvinced about the value of corporate citizenship. The final strand of my argument for the validity of the citizen brand concept therefore requires a theory of the processes by which it works. I touched on one aspect of this in the last chapter when analysing one of the consumer research studies. The next chapter considers it in more depth.

A MODEL FOR CITIZEN BRANDS

CHAPTER 4

A MODEL FOR CITIZEN BRANDS

Why it Works

*T*he previous three chapters have discussed, and I hope demonstrated, the correlation between citizenship, branding and business performance and then some of the historical baggage that restricts objective analysis of it. But there remains an outstanding question: Why does being a citizen brand result in greater business success?

A major criticism of corporate citizenship as an issue has always been that there is no coherent 'model' of why it is linked to commercial success. Without a 'model' – a concrete explanation of the processes involved – citizenship appears in the boardroom as a fuzzy, woolly, 'nice-to-have', rather than a pragmatic, sensible, 'must-have'. This chapter aims to redress that by describing the process by which I believe it works. I touched on this in Chapter 2 when discussing some of the consumer research studies but here I expand on the model to provide an integrated explanation of how the process operates.

This is no easy task for two reasons. First, a broad range of diverse issues is involved. How, for example, can you have a model that includes such factors as environmental consciousness, work-life balance, fair trade policies and concerns about third world poverty? This all-embracing approach not only tends to 'clutter' the argument – as it includes so much – but it tends to undermine it too through the breadth of its claims. How can one process achieve all these things?

It also raises the spectre of political agendas being pursued underneath the banner of corporate citizenship. For example, different advocacy or pressure groups might be tempted to promote their own specific aims under the more general, larger, and therefore legitimizing, umbrella of corporate responsibility. So, environmentalists rub shoulders with employment rights activists, art supporters with human rights campaigners.[1]

Second the process is complex and difficult to track and the direct impact hard to measure, raising similar problems to those encountered in the analysis of advertising. Thus, the breadth and complexity of the issue potentially undermines its credibility.

But, in fact the whole process can be described more simply. There are, I believe, two specific factors that explain why corporate citizenship leads to improved commercial success: one that incorporates all those activities that lead to *direct* and measurable impacts; and one that involves *indirect* and less easily measurable impacts. The term citizen brand incorporates both aspects although in the context of this book it is the indirect element that is most important as it goes to the heart of my contention about the relationship between citizenship and branding. Being less direct and harder to measure does not mean that it is any less important.

For this reason I will limit my discussion of the direct impacts to an overview and some brief examples, in order to concentrate on the indirect component. In reality the distinction between the two is not as clear cut as I would like, as I point out later, but I do believe it helps in understanding and describing the processes involved.

DIRECT IMPACTS

What do I mean by direct impacts? Here I am referring to specific initiatives, that can be categorized as environmentally or socially responsible behaviour, that have been implemented precisely for their environmental or social impact but which also result in tangible commercial benefits. The major components are as follows.

Environmental Initiatives

There are at least three reasons why taking account of environmental concerns is linked with commercial success. First, it can be a catalyst for change, leading to innovative and more productive solutions. Here, there is considerable evidence that taking a more environmentally conscious approach leads to improved efficiency. An example is Dow Chemicals' new environmental equipment and programmes that had an expected return on investment of between 30 and 40 per cent, as I noted in Chapter 1. Second, in today's climate (no pun intended) companies that are environmentally aware are deemed to be less risky to investors.[2] In part, of course, this is an indirect impact too as it relates to the overall perception of the company and its brand equity but I include it here as there is a documented direct correlation. Third, there is the direct impact on consumer behaviour. The most obvious example of this is when consumers seek out or reject a company or product because of its environmental credentials.

Employment Issues

Many studies have shown the direct benefits – in terms of greater commitment, motivation and productivity – to be gained from an investment in human capital. Whether it be a clear set of core values that workers can relate to (Collins and Porras),[3] an attention to basic working conditions or looking more broadly at how work fits in with people's lives outside work, all can directly impact on a company's success. Sometimes, as in the case of allowing, or even encouraging, flexible working, it might appear that initiatives like these generate costs with no consequent payback in productivity and profitability. But this has been shown to be a simplistic and incorrect analysis – example after example has shown that flexible work hours, job sharing and the like produce real bottom line benefits. Helping workers to get a better work–life balance invariably helps the company too.[4]

Suppliers

In a world of outsourcing and 'just-in-time' processes, the role of suppliers is crucial. As with employees, understanding supplier needs and concerns and developing an open, mutually beneficial relationship often leads to a more fruitful and productive association. Trust is a critical issue here and those companies that maintain long-term trusting relationships with their suppliers are likely to be rewarded with better, more flexible service. The success of Japanese car companies in the 1980s was in part the result of their close links with their suppliers. Talking to suppliers about their own corporate citizen behaviour can have its benefits too. For example, they might be persuaded to install a more environmentally friendly production process that is, in fact, more efficient and hence more profitable for them, while reducing costs for you. In this way, companies can push corporate citizenship and good business practice down the supply chain to mutual advantage.

Community Involvement

Companies can gain from investing in the communities in which their offices or manufacturing plants are based. Clearly, through employment they can impact directly on the well-being of not only individuals but the community as a whole, particularly where they are the major employer. But through other broader initiatives (for example, links with, and support for, local schools) they can generate goodwill that not only improves the motivation and loyalty of their employees but encourages the support and help of the wider community too. It can also have the direct impact of improving the physical environment for local employees and their families and the skill and the cultural base from which future workers can be drawn. For example, Ford Motor Company has not only built a new manufacturing facility at its Maraimalai Nagar plant in India, but a new local school too. By doing this and providing teachers as well, it is investing in the future well-being and cohesiveness of the locality and moreover in the future pool of human resources. Of all the areas of direct impact this one is most like the enlightened, self-interested philanthropy of the past, particularly where it is applied to developing economies. The parallels, for instance, between Ford's activity in India in the twenty-first century and Cadbury's in Birmingham in the nineteenth are pronounced. The difference is that nowadays not only is the local community concerned about what the company is doing in these localities, but so is part of the wider consumer base too. Companies like Nike (and other manufacturers accused of exploiting the third world's labour force) have found this out to their cost.

Broader Social and Ethical Issues

Even an interest in broader social and ethical issues like animal welfare and fair trade can have a direct impact on a company's commercial performance in at least two ways. First, as with the specific issue of environmental concern, consumers may favour or boycott companies as a result of their activities in this area. So, for example, some people choose Body Shop specifically because of its stance on animal testing. This can work the other way too, and for companies who do not even deal directly with consumers. The sorry tale of the British pharmaceutical research company Huntingdon Life Sciences makes the point. Thanks to animal rights activists sending bomb threats to Philips and Drew, the fund manager sold its 11 per cent stake in the company at a cut-down price and Huntingdon's share price remains depressed.[5] A recent MORI survey for the Co-operative Bank[6] illustrates the potentially positive (people actively buying) and negative (people deliberately boycotting) impact on consumer behaviour. While this may overestimate the real effect, it suggests that a significant minority of consumers are regularly (in this case at least four times a year) buying or not buying on the basis of perceptions about the company's ethical behaviour (Figure 4.1).

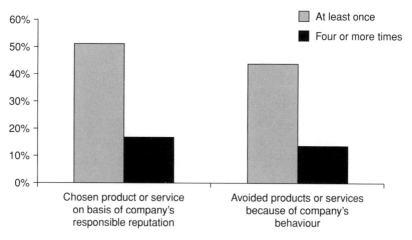

Figure 4.1   Impact of social and ethical issues on consumer behaviour. Proportion agreeing to each statement.

Source: Research conducted by MORI for the Co-operative Bank's report, *Who are the Ethical Consumers?*, 2000.

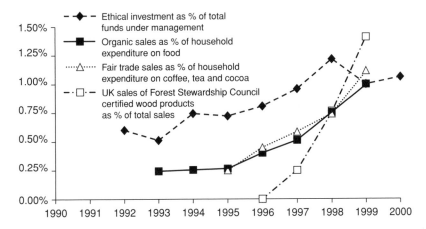

Figure 4.2 Growth in sales of ethical products. Each product's share of its market.

Source: Research conducted by New Economics Foundation for the Co-operative Bank's report, *Who are the Ethical Consumers?*, 2000.

Work by the New Economics Foundation, also for the Co-operative Bank,[7] shows how consumer interest in such issues is translating into real sales, as opposed to stated opinion in market research surveys. Specific ethical products currently only take a small proportion of any market. For example, fair trade sales as a proportion of household expenditure on coffee, tea and cocoa accounts for only just over 1 per cent. But, as the Foundation notes 'in certain key areas, market share is considerably higher' to the extent that 'Cafédirect fairly traded roast and ground coffee now has 5% of the market . . . and is growing at 9% a year'. Importantly, as Figure 4.2 shows, although still small in market share terms, they are growing rapidly.

The second reason why business should take an interest in broader social issues is that companies, and the larger ones specifically, benefit from a thriving, stable and cohesive society. To take one example, lower crime rates are likely to mean not only less direct crime against business (like shoplifting) but also a more secure high street and shopping environment for customers and employees.

This is the point John Banham was making when he talked of 'an increasingly deprived, resentful and repressed minority'[8] as I noted in the last chapter. Do companies like BT want their telephone kiosks vandalized or Marks and Spencer their shops? Does McDonalds want rough sleepers begging outside their restaurants or Starbucks to have bricks thrown through its windows? Of course not. And for large companies with a mass market appeal the more people who can afford their products the better. Reduced poverty can lead directly to increased sales. Indeed, in mature, saturated markets it may be the only way to growth. Some business executives understand this point:

> it is in our company's interest that we have thriving inner cities, and that people have a healthy diet.

> if we work in a healthy, prosperous, growing society, we're going to do better.[9]

British Telecom, which has a dominant position in the UK market for fixed line telecommunications services recognizes this in particular:

> BT's continued success depends on the skills and the resources of our people, the loyalty of our customers and the health and prosperity of the communities of which we are part. *Successful companies need successful communities.*[10] [My emphasis]

So too does Marks and Spencer:

> By supporting those communities where we operate we bring added value, create safer living and working environments, better educated young people, more effective small businesses, an enriched cultural life and a healthier nation. In turn, this creates a more prosperous and self-sufficient society, which is obviously good for business. *Put simply, healthy back streets lead to healthy high streets.*[11] [My emphasis]

Meanwhile, Jac Nasser, president and chief executive officer of Ford sees one of his most important jobs as being to ensure that the company is 'doing good in the communities that we are in, be it the environment, education or helping out the society that we're doing business with'.[12]

INTELLIGENT BUSINESS

All these factors also have one other direct impact on companies, one that is, if anything, the most important of all – the provision of *business intelligence*. By engaging in these issues and activities, businesses inevitably develop a broader, more outward-looking view of their operating environment. They understand better the world they operate in and their relationship with it. There are many benefits from this: better market research; faster anticipation of potential problems and quicker reactions to them; to name but a few. In this sense, corporate citizenship becomes another form of market intelligence. This is, in effect, a reconfiguration of a standard exhortation of management gurus: inwardly focused companies struggle; outwardly focused ones thrive.

All of these initiatives are consistent with basic good management practice. They all contain elements of some of the major themes of current management theories as espoused by some of the most respected commentators and 'gurus' of today. The likes of Tom Peters and Robert Waterman,[13] or Gary Hamel and C. K. Prahalad[14] and, of course, the giant of them all Peter Drucker[15] all highlight the importance of one or more of:

- innovation
- employees as most valuable assets
- customer focus
- supply chain management
- flexibility
- and being an externally focused company.

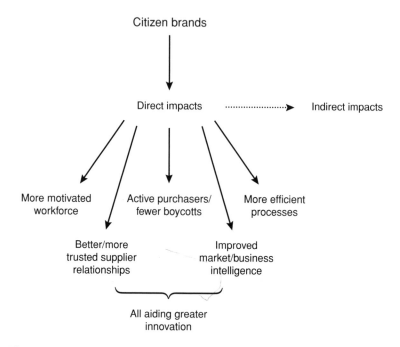

Figure 4.3   Direct impacts on commercial success. Schematic representation.

Source: Michael Willmott/Future Foundation.

Being a good corporate citizen in the way that I have described it, and in the examples I have given, is an aid to all these. In that sense, the concept of citizen brands encompasses, and is consistent with, the very best of current management thinking.

These factors and their direct impacts are illustrated in Figure 4.3. Note, though, that the commercial implications do not end there. These issues also feed into the less clearly defined, but no less important, indirect impact of citizenship – the core concept of citizen brands itself.

INDIRECT IMPACTS

Corporate citizenship feeds indirectly into commercial success via the mechanism of branding. In many ways, this is the most powerful aspect of citizen brands but is, at the same time, the most difficult to prove. In this, it is much like advertising.

Debate has raged for years about how and why advertising works and continues to do so. Yet, it is not only an integral part of commercial activity that is almost universally used by business but expenditure on it has also been growing in real terms for many decades. But people are far from clear why, and even whether, it works and thus whether the expenditure is justified. The old adage 'half the money I spend on advertising is wasted, and the trouble is I don't know which half' has as much resonance today as it did when it was first espoused many years ago.[16]

In fact, there is now a body of research that does allow a plausible model of the advertising process to be developed. From this, we can begin to understand why some advertising works and some does not. Mike Hall, former planning director at Leagas Delaney in London and now Group Chief Executive of Hall and Partners has developed a theoretical model of how advertising works. Initially based on research among practitioners and users of advertising in 1990,[17] Hall has developed the model further over the ensuing years through his own experience in providing advertising research services.[18] The success of his company in that time is a testament to the plausibility and relevance of the model – certainly in the eyes of his clients. Put briefly, Hall proposes that rather than there being one model of how advertising works, there are in fact four major ones (and a number of sub-models that I will not elaborate upon here). These are:

- *The sales response model* – this is where advertising seeks short-term changes in consumer behaviour. It stimulates direct interest in (and hence sales of) a brand but does little in terms of brand building. Advertising in this vein might be price-led or involve a special offer; it might just be reminding people that now is a good time to buy a product. Hall argues that in terms of chronology this was the first model of advertising.

■ *The persuasion model* – here, the role of advertising is to persuade consumers about the brand's functional superiority. It assumes that people will not buy the brand unless they believe it will solve a problem or that it performs better than others. A typical ad here would be 'this washes whiter' or 'this goes faster'. This model evolved as brands and mass consumer markets developed from the 1950s onwards.

■ *The involvement model* – the purpose here is to get consumers to buy into the brand values. This is not that the product necessarily performs better but that it stands for something that the consumer wants to be associated with. As Hall notes, these values could be ones such as 'pride, male bonding, caring, fun, excitement and contemporaneity' so the advertising would be about what the brand stands for or who uses it. This model developed from the mid-1960s onwards.

■ *The salience model* – this is the newest and most radical model according to Hall and dates from the 1980s and 1990s. The attempt here is to get consumers interested in the brand not because it performs better, nor because it has complementary values but because it stands out: it is radically different, it is big, it is self-assured. Barclays Bank's advertising campaign in Britain in 2000 was an example of this. We are *big* it said.[19]

Hall argues that although the different models have developed at different times in response to different needs, all four remain relevant today. It is worth quoting him at length, not least because it helps to clarify further the difference between the models:

> just because there are four different models of how advertising works, you don't have to choose just one of them. Not even for the same brand. Because a brand has different objectives for different targets

at different times. BA [British Airways] wrote ads to a Persuasion model for its First Class seat that turns into a bed, to an Involvement model based around Club World, and to a Salience model to raise its overall status. But it also uses Sales Response ads even if you can't clip a coupon to take up the offer.[20]

This also explains why some advertising does not work. If you use the wrong advertising for the wrong purpose then you will not achieve the success you expected.

More important for the concept of citizen brands (as I discuss later) is that even though all the advertising models are still relevant, the balance is moving from the sales response and persuasion ones (the traditional perception of advertising) towards the 'newer' models of involvement and salience. Certainly, all the social and economic trends that I discuss later would be consistent with this.

To this model of how advertising works, I would add two more general points which help to explain how it indirectly benefits a company. First, a company that can afford to advertise, and certainly those that can advertise on television, must be reasonably big, so the very fact they are advertising sends a certain message to the market. Indeed, some people have argued that this is the main reason why advertising works. For instance, economist John Kay, who was Dean of Oxford University Business School, suggested that advertising is seldom informative or persuasive but works because it tells the consumer that the advertiser is committed to the product and the market – why else would they spend so much money?

> Much advertising – indeed all of the most conspicuous and costly advertising – is neither informative or persuasive . . . the only information such advertising conveyed was that the advertiser spent a lot of money on advertising. But . . . this is useful information. It tells you that the advertiser is committed to the market and the product . . . And if [the advertiser] is committed to the product and the market, it also makes sense to devote resources to ensuring the quality of the product.[21]

This may seem like Hall's salience model but in fact it is different. Here, the advertising itself is not saying the company is big; it is the very fact that advertising has taken place (which might be directed towards a persuasion model, for example) that is.

The second, more general reason why I believe advertising benefits business is that it encourages companies to *take a more external focus on their business*. Since the development of advertising planning in the 1960s, trying to understand potential customers' needs and the environment they operate in is now an explicit part of the development of the communications strategy.

This might be the theory of how advertising works but what evidence is there to support the thesis? Certainly, my own experience in this area – having observed a number of econometric projects that sought to develop sales forecasting models – is mixed. More often than not the level of advertising expenditure had no discernible impact on sales. But two criticisms can be made of this. First, as I have just noted, not all advertising should be, or is, focused directly at immediate sales increases. Second, the impact of advertising may not be direct but, instead, indirect – and the indirect process may be rather complex.

Recent research by the British Institute of Practitioners in Advertising (IPA) not only confirms this but also provides persuasive evidence that advertising works.[22] The study involved a special analysis from the celebrated PIMS database[23] of over 200 companies mainly operating in branded consumer products in Europe. There were two main conclusions from the research. The first was that it is not absolute advertising but relative spend compared to competitors that is most important. Second was that 'the correlation between advertising and profitability is not direct but indirect'.[24] Both points again help to explain the failure of some econometric analyses in this area.

The indirect process by which advertising works is through the mechanism of superior customer value. Previous analysis of the whole of the PIMS database has shown this to be 'a prime

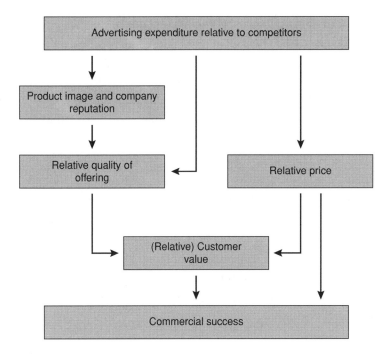

Figure 4.4   How advertising indirectly affects sales and profits. Schematic representation.

Source: Adapted from *How Advertising Impacts on Profitability*. PIMS database/Institute of Practitioners in Advertising.

driver of growth and profitability'.[25] Customer value is a function of perceived quality and price relative to others. Advertising can affect both of these: price through the sales response model and quality through the persuasion model. But the IPA analysis also showed that perceptions of quality could not only be affected directly by advertising but also indirectly via perceptions of product image and reputation. Advertising would influence these through the involvement and salience models. The relationships are shown in Figure 4.4.

CITIZEN BRANDS AND MODELS OF ADVERTISING

Readers may wonder why I have spent some time discussing the processes by which advertising impacts on a company's reputation and commercial success. The reason is that there are extraordinary parallels with the concept of citizen brands.

For a start, we can see that the idea of citizenship relates specifically to the involvement model. That model stresses the values of companies and brands and the desire of consumers to associate with them. Hall argues that the importance of this model is increasing as such values become more important to consumers. I argue that some of the most important of these values will be those surrounding citizenship.

Then, both advertising and corporate citizenship help businesses by encouraging, indeed even forcing, them to take a more external focus.

Finally, there are striking similarities between the model of the process by which advertising works and the one that I developed independently for corporate citizenship (see Chapter 2). The IPA model provides evidence that advertising can improve product image and company reputation which in turn influences perceptions of quality. This then leads to a perception of increased value and hence higher sales and profitability. My model of citizen brands presents evidence that corporate citizenship (as well as transparency and, to a lesser extent, communications activity) helps to increase trust in the company. This is related to higher satisfaction and leads to enhanced customer retention and, implied by that, greater commercial success.

It can be seen that in structure the models are incredibly similar. Exchange a few phrases – trust for reputation, satisfaction for perceived value, loyalty for market share – and the two have effectively the same form. The difference is that one is looking at advertising, the other at corporate citizenship. The activities are different, the processes the same.

Figure 4.5 A coherent model of citizen brands. Schematic representation.

Source: Michael Willmott/Future Foundation.

So, alongside the direct impact that corporate citizenship has on business success, we can now see how it generates an indirect impact. If we return to the figure on direct impacts we can add the indirect model as well (Figure 4.5).

Beyond the direct effects, being a citizen brand helps to build reputation and trust. This has two impacts. First, as in the advertising model, this has the general impact of increasing perceptions about the quality of the company's products and service. Second, it creates what you might call a 'goodwill' bank – a depth of feeling for the company that will make customers more disposed towards it, even to the extent that they might overlook occasional lapses. Both of these lead to increased loyalty and higher value and more profitable customers.

This is my interpretation of the results shown in Chapter 2 where trust was correlated to satisfaction (that in the context of this chapter I have taken to mean the same as 'perceived quality/value') but also, and independently, to loyalty itself. To put this another way, the relationship between corporate citizenship, trust and loyalty is important in two ways. First, because customers trust you, they are less likely to look elsewhere in the first place (satisfaction/quality). Second, if you do make a mistake they are more likely to forgive you (goodwill).

All this reinforces the idea that, in fact, corporate citizenship is becoming a crucial part of branding: citizenship is an integral part of brand equity. Furthermore, all the evidence is that it is likely to grow in importance as a branding issue. As differentiation on basic factors becomes harder (the satisfaction element) then differentiation will focus more on the other aspects affecting loyalty: trust, citizenship and transparency. This is certainly consistent with the changing emphasis of advertising over the last few decades that has seen a shift from the persuasion model to those of involvement and salience.

This raises the important question of why companies embrace advertising but are less enthusiastic about corporate citizenship? This is not true of all businesses though. One major British retailer that I interviewed has already recognized the importance of this by diverting some of the existing marketing expenditure to this new aspect of branding:

> We think it [corporate citizenship] is so important we've devoted a significant part of our marketing budget to it.[26]

But this remains a minority view. As far as I can tell, few companies are currently investing in, or even recognize, the importance of corporate citizenship to branding and commercial success. I hope this chapter has done something to change that because the concept of citizen brands is going to become more important in the future. The evidence to support that proposition is what I turn to next.

PEACE AND PLENTY

CHAPTER 5

PEACE AND PLENTY

Understanding the Impact of the New Political Economy

*I*f I have shown that the concept of citizen brands is already an important one for companies, why has the issue emerged in the way it has? What are the social, economic, political and technological factors that have made this more important than it was ten, twenty or thirty years ago? And will these factors continue to exert an influence in the future increasing the importance of citizenship to companies?

In this section I consider these questions to assess not only why these new citizenship pressures on companies are developing but also to contemplate what sort of future society business will be operating in. In this first chapter I describe the new political economy that is emerging as a result of the twin forces of globalization and economic growth. In the next chapter I look at the technological revolution before turning in subsequent chapters to specific aspects of consumer change: coping with discretion and choice; increasing hysteria and cynicism; and greater volatility in consumer behaviour.

WELCOME TO THE DOOMSAYERS

It is very fashionable nowadays to decry modern society. Every week, in newspapers, magazines, on television and on radio someone is bemoaning the loss of a world where people were happier, communities were stronger, families were more united, the pace of life was more relaxed and so on. You name it, and some pundit will claim that life was better in the past. What is staggering about these claims is that there is so little firm evidence to back them up.

For example, on the front cover of Oliver James' book *Britain on the Couch*[1] is the question 'why are we unhappier than we were in the 1950s – despite being richer?' Yet, there is no objective evidence that we are, in fact, any less happy (whatever that means) than we were in the past. Happiness, of course, is a very difficult thing to measure. What exactly does it involve? Is it not a relative concept, with people judging their happiness by reference to their contemporaries, therefore making comparisons over time difficult? Despite these problems, there has been an attempt to assess whether happiness levels have changed. Professor Andrew Oswald at the University of Warwick has analysed cross-national data covering the last 30 years in Europe and 50 years in America.[2] His conclusions are that:

> Happiness with life seems to be increasing in the USA.

> Since the early 1970s, reported levels of satisfaction with life in European countries has on average risen slightly.

Oswald notes that there is no evidence that growing incomes increase happiness, supporting the idea that happiness is, inevitably, relative. But equally there is no support for the contention that people despite being richer are generally more miserable.

Another doomsayer example is the work of American economist Juliet Schor, famous for her two books *The Overworked American*[3] and *The Overspent American*.[4] Schor's argument in the first book is that Americans are working longer hours, leading to a range of detrimental impacts. However, in a rather damning critique of her analysis, John Robinson and Geoffrey Godbey assert that Schor's claims 'are not supported by diary data'. This would not matter so much except that Schor's analysis was based on their own time-diary data and it was, they claim, selective and partial use:

> Schor uses our time-diary data only for 1975, and then mixes those data with time-estimate data – *a step we question* ... She *does not* use our 1965 time-diary data – the major benchmark year for our analyses ... She also *does not* take into account our time-diary data and published articles from the 1985 study.[5] [My emphasis]

They conclude, in a rather understated way, that 'our results and conclusions about trends in hours spent at work are notably different from Schor's'.

Robert H. Frank effectively repeats Schor's contention in his book *Luxury Fever: Why Money Fails to Satisfy in an Era of Success*:[6]

> All of us, rich and poor alike ..., are spending more time at the office and taking shorter vacations; we are spending less time with our families and friends; and we have less time for sleep, exercise, travel, reading and other activities that help maintain body and soul.

Yet, there is no evidence from the United States or Britain that people are sleeping less: 'sleep data show the least variance across time. While many people claim they are so busy that they forgo hours of sleep, little evidence of decreased sleep appears [from the data]'.[7] Professor Jonathan Gershuny's data on sleep highlights a similar conclusion for Britain,[8] while at the same time showing that parents are spending *more time* on child care than they have ever done[9] (Figure 5.1).

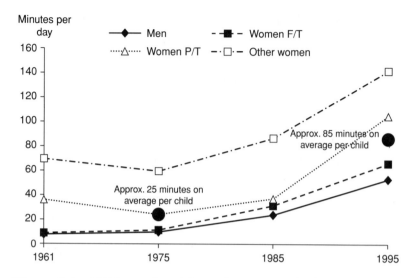

Figure 5.1   Child care time. Men and women with children under 16 (UK).

Source: Jonathan Gershuny with special analysis by Michael Willmott.

Of course the world has changed and not for the better in every single case. But, by and large and by most objective measures things have improved. The refusal to accept these objective facts and to search with fervour for some sign of decline or impending doom may be an underlying human trait. As Brown and Duguid note:

> Since the nineteenth century when the economist Thomas Malthus gloomily predicted that the geometric growth of population would outstrip the arithmetic growth in resources, predictions appear regularly that humanity is on the verge of destroying itself.[10]

Unfortunately, even respected British forecasting organizations are prone to this. Here were some typical comments that marked the end of the millennium:

> Although the economic outlook was bright, the problems facing society at the end of the second millennium were likely to deteriorate by the start of the third.

The ageing population and increased mobility, together with the increase in single-person households and rising stress levels at home and at work, have all led to increasing isolation for many people.[11]

This last point is a highly contentious one as all the research shows that people are going out and socializing more, have more people in their homes and to dinner and, thanks to the new technologies (see next chapter), are communicating more than ever before.

Although doomsayers have been around throughout history the discrepancy between the reality and the hype has probably never been greater (certainly in the advanced economies of the developed world). Thus, the critical issue for business and politicians alike is not really people's unhappiness or poverty or ill-health but rather, it is in understanding the impact of a stable and prosperous society on people's values and behaviour. This includes understanding when and where the misplaced perception of decline is relevant and when and where it is not.

PEACE AND PLENTY

This phenomenon of 'peace and plenty' – as Jim Murphy[12] has described it – is, I believe, a crucial one in the development of citizen brands because it does impact on consumer values and the political environment. The argument goes as follows.

Despite the doom and gloom suggested by many commentators we currently live in unprecedented times. The end of the cold war and the collapse of communism – hailed at the time as a momentous event – has turned out to be just that. Diverted, almost as soon as it happened, by an economic slowdown in the western world (and recession in some countries like the United States and Britain) it is my view that we have underestimated just what impact this has had on the economics and psychology of today. The peace dividend is a reality: military spending diminished from 11 per cent of UK government spending in 1987 to

7 per cent in 1998,[13] releasing money for increased spending on social security and health. This is a very real and measurable impact. But more important in my view, but less quantifiable, is the psychological impact it has had. Speak to children under the age of 10 or 15 even and they have no comprehension of the underlying fear that accompanies the idea of nuclear war. In the 1999 film *Blast from the Past* a government scientist builds his own bunker and, believing a missile attack to have started during the Cuban missile crisis takes his family down into it, to re-emerge 30 years later. A colleague's 10 year old daughter on seeing the film said she had no idea that there had ever been that sort of threat or fear – it was the first time she had been confronted with the idea of mass destruction.

I think we forget how pervasive and deeply ingrained our concerns about nuclear war were. Since the 1970s social and market research company MORI has asked the general public what they think is the most important issue facing Britain. Even in the 1980s, disarmament/nuclear war nearly always ranked in the top three issues with sometimes as many as 40 per cent saying it was the most important problem the country faced. From 1988 the numbers choosing this option began to decline dramatically. Now, it is the most important worry for only 1 per cent of the population.[14] The Future Foundation has repeated part of a survey carried out by the market research firm Taylor Nelson Sofres during the 1980s.[15] One question gave respondents a list of five ambitions and asked them which one they would choose if they had one wish. In the 1980s the population's first choice by a long way was 'less fear', selected by around 45 per cent. By 1999 it was down to a mere 15 per cent, now only the third choice (see Figure 5.2). At first, I could not understand this result given the increasing neuroses about crime and safety (see Chapter 8). But now I believe it merely reflects the removal of the biggest threat of all – nuclear war.

What has been the reaction to this? Well, arguably one has been either to substitute other fears for the old ones or to discover

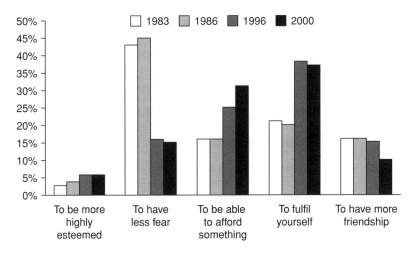

Figure 5.2   Less fear more fulfilment? 'If you had just one wish, which one of these would you choose?'

Source: *n*Vision/Future Foundation.

new ones. So, people worry more about crime and disease and about community and family. We now have a new global threat too – environmental degradation and global warming. I am not saying there are not legitimate environmental concerns – indeed, I think there are – but rather that, with the threat of nuclear war diminished, there is a natural tendency to concentrate on other potentially catastrophic events. An important point though is that these new threats are longer-term ones. Global warming is not going to bring disaster literally tomorrow as nuclear war could.

But if these are conflated concerns with a less immediate effect then surely the importance of them to people, and people's behaviour, will be more variable? And that is exactly what has happened – concern about environmental issues has fluctuated, often in tune with the economic cycle. Concerns they may be, but they are less deeply ingrained and, importantly, less immediately personally threatening.

Look again at Figure 5.2. If the response 'less fear' has gone down, what has increased? A number of areas have gone up: 'to

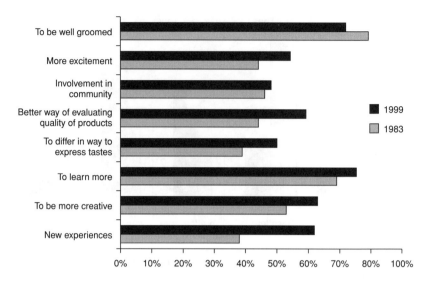

Figure 5.3   The growth of individualism. Proportion feeling a strong or moderate need for . . .

Source: *n*Vision/Future Foundation.

be more highly esteemed', for example. But the two big gainers are 'to be able to afford something' and – now the number one wish – 'to fulfil yourself'. A separate question from the same survey found more people wanting new experiences, more excitement and to fulfil oneself by being more creative (Figure 5.3). In the absence of cold war concerns people have become more worried about their own personal development – about what threatens them as individuals or what they, as individuals, can do to improve their life. The reduction of solid global threats has helped to boost the growth of individualism.

Of course, military conflicts still exist. But nowadays these are against less powerful, less well-equipped regimes like Iraq or Serbia. Although much was made at the time of the potential use of biological weapons in the Gulf War, the reality was a military mismatch – Iraq never had a chance against the might of the Western military machine. This, as we saw in Kosovo, has now become a new type of war – at least for us in the West. Laser guided bombs and cruise missiles weave their way precisely to their military targets. While some innocent civilians 'over there' may be casualties as the odd missile goes astray or intelligence wrongly identifies targets and while huge, and long-term, hardship is caused by the destruction of infrastructure, civilians at home are not threatened at all. Indeed, if the past few 'wars' are any-thing to go by, the risks faced by our military personnel are pretty slim too, and the potential for public outcry limited. This is a sanitized version of war for the West – more an entertainment (as we receive round the clock, live news coverage) than a threat.

For the developed world, Vietnam was the last serious 'body bag' war where not only regulars, but conscripts were involved. But in the 1970s and 1980s the threat of nuclear war remained. Only now, and for the first time in history, do we in the West have a generation of people who have never experienced the fear that accompanies the prospect of them or their loved ones going to war or of their country being decimated by it. That is unprecedented indeed.

NEVER HAD IT SO GOOD?

If the threat of major wars and nuclear destruction has receded, are there not broader economic problems facing people, and specifically that of poverty? Certainly, one of the more obvious economic trends in a number of western economies over the last two decades has been the increasing polarization of incomes. This is most noticeable in some of the Anglo-Saxon economies that have most readily embraced free market capitalism, like the USA and Britain. Although most people view this as a bad development, with increasing numbers wanting a fairer distribution (see Figure 5.4), the argument is not quite as simple as it might seem.

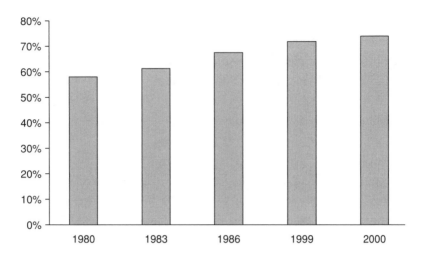

Figure 5.4   Support for a fairer division of wealth. Proportion who agree that 'there should be a fairer division of wealth and money'.

Source: *n*Vision/Future Foundation.

First, although incomes are undoubtedly being distributed less equitably, practically everyone is better off in real terms – it is just that the richer are getting richer, faster. So the question is one about relative, rather than real poverty since more people can afford some of the basic, and not so basic, items of life. A passage from Melvin Bragg's novel *The Soldier's Return* emphasizes the point:

> the inhabitants of the Rabbit Warren at the very centre of town were to be sent almost a mile away, to the south, into houses with three, sometimes four, bedrooms and an indoor lavatory and even a bath, with gardens front and back and no damp, no TB, no rats, no cockroaches, no chesty coughs, no beatings and worse, no stench of beasts and excrement in the street.[16]

Compared with the past the living conditions of nearly everyone are much better now. The 'problem' is that as living standards improve, so expectations increase. In the post-war period that Bragg was writing about many people did not have an indoor toilet and to have one was deemed, if not a luxury, then certainly a movement away from poverty, deprivation and misery. There was no mention then of a refrigerator, but nowadays this is considered an essential item to have according to a recent study by the Joseph Rowntree Foundation.[17] Indeed to not have one, is considered a measure of deprivation. This is the paradox of growth: although people's material conditions compared with the past improve; their condition relative to others might not. They are on one measure better off, but they might not feel it.

This is not to say that the concept of relative poverty should be dismissed – it is clearly an important aspect of social well-being and cohesion (although, there is an argument that to achieve cohesion there needs to be a recognition of the individualism and diversity in modern culture).[18] If the gap in financial terms between different groups in society becomes too great then alienation and social unrest might result – something that would not be in the interest of the corporate sector. But the idea of relative poverty also has its problems. For a start, one measure of relative poverty – the proportion of people with less than 50 per cent of average incomes – tends to decrease in a recession. The reason is that if, as you would expect, the average income declines as the economy turns down, then the level at which you are deemed to be in poverty goes down too. The result can be that fewer people are below the threshold – fewer people are deemed to be poor. This is misleading as we know that recessions always cause greater hardship and particularly for those on lower incomes.

There is another question about relative poverty: relative to what? Most measures concentrate on comparisons with other people in the same country. But, as globalization continues and, in Europe, the integration of markets grows then is this the best measure? For example, the poor in Britain could in theory fall further behind the better-off citizens in their own country but become less poor in relation to Europe as a whole. This is important because your views about this could directly influence national economic policy. This can be shown by way of illustration. Assume, for simplicity's sake, that a government has two policy options:

1. provides reduced income growth in comparison to global
    competitors and a worse relative position for the poorer groups
    compared to poorer groups in other countries but with *decreased
    income polarization* within the country;
2. provides greater growth than in other countries which means
    on a global scale the poorer groups are better off than similar
    groups in other countries but with *increased income polarization*
    within the country.

In posing this question to people, I have been surprised how
many have chosen option 1 – they would rather people are poorer
(in global terms) but more equal nationally, than better off and
less equal. In other words in the western world this is as much a
debate about inequality as it is about poverty. In an era of peace
and plenty it is relatives not absolutes that matter.

My point here is not to belittle the fact that poverty still exists
in what are, in world-wide terms, very rich countries – nor that
strenuous efforts should not be made to help those in such straits.
It is not that excessive executive pay (and pay-offs to corporate
managers who are sacked for failure or incompetence) is acceptable. These are important problems that any civilized society should
address. However, despite this, it is an inescapable fact that the
majority of citizens in industrialized economies are much better
off in real terms than their parent's generation and – and this is
the critical fact – have reached a level of discretionary spending
that has taken them on to a new level. Of course, despite real
income increases most people still do not have as much money
or possessions as they might like. If they recognize that they cannot
be as rich as Bill Gates or Richard Branson, or Michael Jordan
or David Beckham, they would certainly not mind those possessions or lifestyles just beyond their current means. And, as the
income distribution stretches, more people will aspire to goods or
services they cannot afford. It is noticeable, for example, that the
proportion of people wishing they were able to afford something

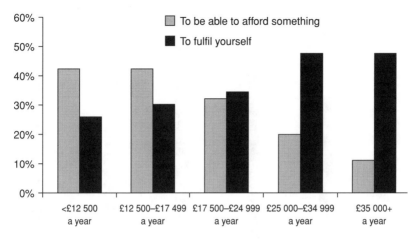

Figure 5.5 Income and aspirations. Proportion choosing certain aspects as main wish by income.

Source: *n*Vision/Future Foundation.

has gone up and is specially high, not surprisingly, for those on lower incomes. Those on higher incomes meanwhile are most likely to seek more fulfilment (Figure 5.5). This, then, is the impact of polarizing incomes: a growth in the search for fulfilment at the same time as, if not yet a growing 'culture of envy',[19] then at least a maintenance of aspirational consumption. (Although some have argued that a mood of anti-materialism is developing, there is precious little evidence of such 'downshifting' – as it is called – actually taking place.)

But all this discussion about aspirations is within the context of a great deal of discretion already available to most people. In much of the developed world, the majority of the population can buy a new car, holiday abroad or own their own home. Effectively every home in Britain has a telephone and a television, nearly all have a washing machine, fridge, video recorder and central heating (see Figure 5.6). New appliances reach high penetration levels in relatively short periods of time nowadays. It took over 50 years for telephones to reach more than 50 per cent of UK homes;

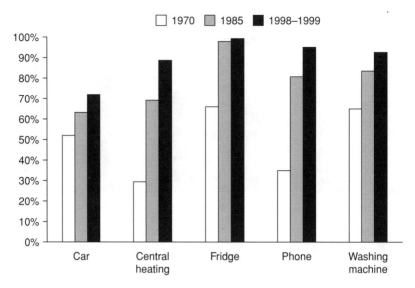

Figure 5.6 Ownership of various household goods. Percentage of households with selected items.

Source: *Family Spending*, National Statistics.

mobile phones have reached 50 per cent of the population in just 12 years. When colour television was launched in 1968 it was 10 years before it reached more than half of households; digital TV, launched in 1998, is forecast by the Future Foundation to get to that point in six years. That is why new concepts like paid for television or the launch of the National Lottery in Britain in 1994 can suddenly appear and devour billions of pounds of consumer expenditure. The majority of people now have an increasing degree of economic discretion.

   People are not only better off in income terms but in wealth too. Considerable assets are held by the public in pension funds, housing, share ownership and saving or deposit accounts. The total net financial wealth held by British households is now over £2000 billion, having increased fourfold in real terms over the last twenty years.[20] More people have a safety net and the typical size of it is larger. Perhaps this is one of the reasons why – despite the general problems and worries that are supposedly so endemic in society – the ownership of life insurance is declining.[21] Do you need insurance when you have sufficient assets to cover the ups and downs of life?

This degree of affluence for the majority has led some to suggest that we are reaching a new stage in society's development. In particular, that we are reaching the self-actualization phase of Maslow's hierarchy of needs.[22] Others have talked of the emergence of a post-material society.

To remind readers, Maslow suggested that as societies develop so people move up the hierarchy from the basic sustenance required just to live of primitive societies through security to socialization, and then through self-esteem to self-actualization (see Figure 5.7). The stage of self-esteem is associated with lifestyles focusing on status driven consumption ('what I have'). Self-actualization is less concerned with appearance and more with personal

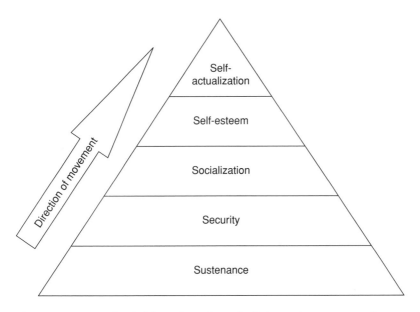

Figure 5.7 Maslow's hierarchy of needs. Schematic representation.
Source: *The Responsible Organisation*, BT/Future Foundation.

development, quality of life ('how I am') and, importantly, with wider concerns.

Whether materialism, as such, has been banished is, as I suggested earlier, debatable. But, it seems to me that there clearly is something in the argument that other, wider concerns, are influencing people in their attitudes and behaviour. Certainly, long-term studies have suggested that more and more people can be categorized as self-actualized or post-materialists.[23]

There is evidence that this does feed through into consumer behaviour and particularly that related to corporate citizenship. For example, Environics[24] developed a survey of attitudes to the role of large companies in society. The 23 countries included ranged from Argentina to Kazakhstan to the United States. When the results are plotted against the GDP per capita a correlation can be see (Figure 5.8). On the whole, the richer a society becomes the more its inhabitants believe that companies have a role in setting ethical standards and in helping build a better society.

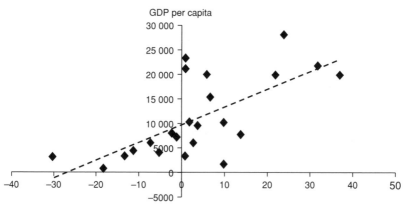

Whether companies should be engaged in setting ethical standards and building a better society
(a positive rating = yes – see note 25)

Figure 5.8 Companies, society and affluence. Belief about the role of companies by Gross Domestic Product per capita.[25]

Source: Environics/The Prince of Wales Business Leaders Forum/The Conference Board/Future Foundation.

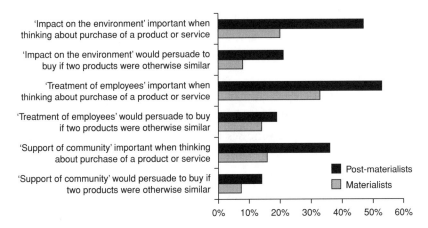

Figure 5.9   Post-materialism and consumption. Proportion saying factor is important when making a purchasing decision/would be persuasive in final choice if price and quality of two products were comparable.

Source: Co-operative Bank/MORI.

Research by MORI in Britain for the Co-operative Bank[26] looked directly at whether people who could be characterized as at the top of the Maslow hierarchy – 'post-materialists'[27] – had different attitudes to corporate behaviour. The results are shown in Figure 5.9 and clearly also suggest that as societies develop, more and more people will be concerned about the citizenship credentials of a business.

THE NEW THREAT – GLOBALIZATION

Within all this discussion of a prosperous industrialized world with fewer real threats and justifiable fears there is one area where people not only feel threatened but where they are clearly directly affected – globalization. Some commentators see globalization as an inherently negative development (see, for example, John Gray,[28] Faux and Mishel[29] and Vandana Shiva[30]). Personally, I feel less strongly about globalization. Indeed, I believe it does ultimately promote economic growth and can be a force for improved social and economic conditions around the world (see, for example, Dollar and Kray).[31] But, at the same time it clearly does impact upon companies, countries and citizens.

The steady deregulation of world trade – through GATT and WTO, as well as within regions such as the European Union or NAFTA – is forcing businesses in all sectors to reassess their operations and cost bases in the face of greater competition in previously protected home markets. Since the Second World War, there have been really three distinct periods of trade growth. From 1950 until the early 1980s trade was steadily growing at an annual rate of one and a half times world output. But it accelerated in the 1980s in a new phase of growth, growing between 1984 and 1993 at nearly double the rate of output. But from the early 1990s it quickened its pace again and since 1994 has been growing at three times world gross domestic product (Figure 5.10).

As markets open 'globally', so supply in virtually any sector can be much better organized and any kind of protective price regime is left vulnerable. We are experiencing this today in the

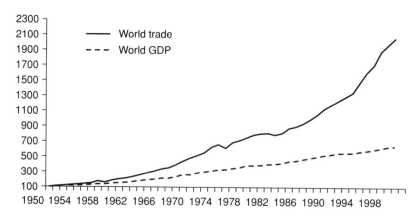

Figure 5.10 The relentless progress of globalization. The growth of world trade versus that of world gross domestic product (index: 1950=100).

Source: World Trade Organisation.

'crisis' of the British farming industry. Price premiums in a number of farming subsectors have been completely eliminated by foreign producers even to the extent that some products cost more per unit for British farmers to produce than they cost the consumer to buy in a supermarket. Similar kinds of pressure are already being felt in drinks retailing, cars, air travel and the like. Globalization allied to low inflation progressively makes unjustified price premiums impossible, in the long run, to protect.

Thus in most market sectors there is a growing need to create and sustain competitive advantage through focusing on core competencies, building strong and valued brands, and keeping costs under control. This is having a major impact on employment and working practices. Down-sizing and the restructuring of corporations, both multinational and national, has resulted in ever more functions being contracted out and a range of more flexible working techniques introduced. Not surprisingly, this has raised concerns about job security.[32]

THE IMPACT ON THE POLITICAL ECONOMY

This, then, is the backdrop to the emerging political economy and a funny mix it is too. Never had it so good, but worried about a range of issues, some unnecessarily and wrongly so. The majority of the people well-off but perhaps feeling less secure in their jobs and increasingly concerned about polarization in society. Globalization driving growth and lowering consumer prices but in a seemingly brutal fashion.

This strange mix has been critical in the emergence of a new political philosophy. First, the reality and seeming inevitability of global competition has forced governments of all political persuasions to adapt in their economic policies to embrace free market competition. At the same time, concern about increased job insecurity and income polarization has been felt to threaten social cohesion and hence has fed the need for policies to address that. This reflects the two poles of the new political economy: full-hearted acceptance of the global market economy while at the same time searching for mechanisms to protect individual citizens from the ravages of it.

Begun by Bill Clinton and recreated by Tony Blair in Britain as 'the third way', it is being adopted in varying degrees by other politicians throughout Europe, most notably Lionel Jospin and Gerhard Schroeder. This is not only a left-of-centre phenomenon. A right-of-centre administration in Spain has followed similar policies and, as Charles Leadbeater has pointed out,[33] George W. Bush presents a similar credo under the guise of 'compassionate conservatism'. Now, Michael Portillo is doing the same from a Conservative perspective in Britain.

This has thrown up some interesting paradoxes. Not least is that those on the left have embraced stable, business friendly, free market economic policies to such an extent that they are seen – at least in Britain and the United States – as safe guardians of the economy in the eyes of Wall Street and the City of London, perhaps even safer than their right-of-centre opponents.

What this new political philosophy is attempting to do is to marry the principles of individual rights, social cohesion and basic welfare with the economic necessity of enterprise and capitalism. What this represents, as American political analyst Mark Lilla[34] has proposed, is the confluence of the economic credo of the 1980s with the social credo of the 1960s – two generations and two political persuasions brought together.

According to Lilla this phenomenon – the 'politics of fusion' as he puts it – explains the general consensus that exists in political debate today. An acceptance of the global market economy (1980s economics) together with support for individual rights and a concern for a degree of social justice (1960s morality). Philip Stephens when discussing Lilla's *New York Review* article summarizes the argument succinctly:

Today's politics, we now know, belongs to conservative liberals and liberal conservatives. These are the politicians who have made their peace with the two big upheavals of the post-war era, the social revolution of the 1960s and its economic counterpart in the 1980s. To win elections in the 1990s you have to be as tolerant of hippies as of yuppies. I hate the phrase, but it is called the politics of inclusion. And it has proved as powerful in the hands of Britain's Tony Blair and Germany's Gerhard Schröder as it has for Mr Clinton.[35]

This may be interesting, but why is it relevant? It is so because this new political economy represents new challenges and new opportunities. Companies and organizations do not operate in a vacuum. To understand some of the implications let us return to Maslow's hierarchy of needs.

It seems to me that this new political philosophy born out of the combined effects of peace and plenty and globalization can be seen as a development of – a step up from – the free market mantra of the 1980s. It is free market, but combined with 1960s style social justice and a concern for individual rights (as Mark Lilla suggested). As a political philosophy, then, it is consistent with the self-actualization phase of Maslow's hierarchy.

An analysis of the predominant corporate structure at times in history suggests that the way business behaves can be linked in a similar way. Thus, in a less developed society, a company's first priority is to provide basic products that people can afford. As society develops, the company takes more notice of its employees, helping to provide security of employment where possible. In British history, this would be reflected in both the development of labour regulations and paternalistic employers (see Chapter 3). As society moves into the socialization phase, then companies begin to produce products and brands that express inclusiveness – in effect the mass market brands of the 1950s and 1960s. The search for status and the development of positional consumption is consistent with the development of designer labels and upmarket brands – arguably, most typified in the 1980s. The movement to

Political ideology

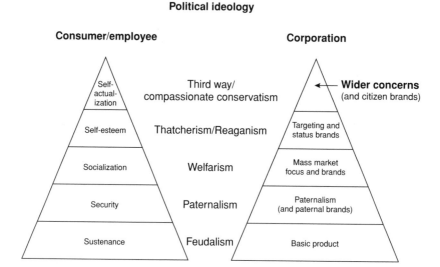

Figure 5.11   Maslow, political economy and corporations. Schematic representation.

Source: Future Foundation.

self-actualization – which, I argued earlier, the more affluent in society are currently engaged in – suggests companies, products and brands should start to embrace a wider perspective, adding to people's personal development and quality of life. To be, in other words, citizen brands.

So, the combined impact of peace and plenty and globalization has profound implications not just for government but for companies too. It may not seem like it yet, but this is potentially a very different political climate to be operating in. This is post-material politics. It is free market economics and, yes, governments are on the whole pro-business but there is a sting in the tail. Governments, and others in society, will expect far more from the corporate sector in the future – companies will be expected not only to be good businesses but good citizens too.

The importance of peace and plenty and globalization is not restricted to its impact on the political economy. It directly affects

consumer attitudes and behaviour and through that has clear implications for companies. I have already discussed the impact of increasing affluence on what might be called 'ethical' consumption. But
there are other outcomes too.

First, and perhaps surprisingly, this new environment makes
consumers *more* demanding. The mix of never had it so good and
increasing concerns and worries makes people expect more. But
most importantly, consumers also feel empowered because most
of them do have a significant degree of discretion. This may seem
strange since I made the point earlier that there has been an
increase in the proportion of people whose main wish is to be
able to afford something. But look at consumer spending growth
in Britain over the last thirty years (Figure 5.12). Those areas
reflecting the basic needs of subsistence and security – food,
housing and energy – have grown but at below average rates. The
more discretionary areas, and the ones that reflect individual
choices – like leisure, clothes or household goods – have grown.
Thus the concern that some people express is – in the termi-
nology I used earlier – not so much about absolutes but about

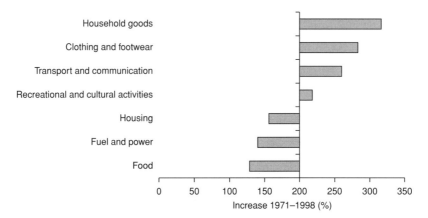

Figure 5.12   Household spending in different sectors. Percentage growth
in real terms, 1971–1988 (all household spending = 200 per cent growth).

Source: National Statistics, author's analysis.

relatives – being able to afford aspirational goods and services rather than necessities. We may wish we could have them but we know we can get by without them. The affluent majority know they have some discretion and they know that they can pick and choose. And thanks to the increasing competition that globalization brings, they know that they can shop around for the best price too.

This is the irony of prosperity: people are price conscious not because they need to be, but because they know they can be. Add to this the unfortunate minority for whom searching for the cheapest price is a necessity and it becomes understandable why there is increased price awareness across, and within, all markets.

So peace and plenty and globalization do not make it any easier for companies, indeed they make life harder. Consumers are more confident (in their dealings with companies), more demanding, more price conscious, while also expecting companies to be good citizens. These trends, together with fears about the negative aspects of globalization, are resulting in an increasing cynicism about business and how it behaves and about multinational companies in particular. This is the reason why the concept of citizen brands is so important. But I discuss this issue of cynicism, and some of the other consumer impacts of peace and plenty in a world of globalization – fear, excess choice and increasing volatility – in later chapters. First I want to consider the other major driver of change in the world at the moment: technology.

BEYOND 'ENDISM'

CHAPTER 6

BEYOND 'ENDISM'

The social side of technology

No book about business, and certainly one that looks at future trends, would be complete without a chapter on new technology.[1] But the hype about the technological revolution is now so great that there is a danger that both the direction and strength of its impact – the when, where and how quickly – is being exaggerated. Certainly, some respected commentators are warning of the perils inherent in an uncritical analysis of the implications of digital technology. John Seely Brown, head of research at the world famous Xerox PARC[2] no less, has in his recent book with Paul Duguid[3] cautioned against the 'endism' inherent in much of contemporary analysis. This is where new technology is predicted to bring about the *end* of mass media, intermediaries, high street retailers and so on.[4] Seely Brown and Duguid go on to describe the myopia of what they call 6-D vision, where the D stands for all those *'futurist-favored'* words beginning with *de-* or *dis-*, such as *demassification, disintermediation* or *disaggregation*. It is not that these two authors deny that there are important developments taking place. They accept that 'particular institutions and particular organizations are under pressure and many will not survive' and that 'none of the D-visions is inherently mistaken or uninteresting'. But, they argue, the analysis and application of it is too linear, too uni-dimensional, too simplistic. They make two specific points: that other 'revolutions' in the past – like the industrial revolution of the last century – have been as dramatic and fast as this one; and that the effects of those revolutions were critically shaped by social forces and that this revolution will be no different. In order to understand the true impact of new technology, they argue, we need to look beyond technology itself and consider social aspects.

There is a lot of sense in what John Seely Brown and Paul Duguid say.[5] The argument that previous revolutions have been as dramatic is a popular and legitimate one. Is the pace of change really any greater now than that experienced in the major historical revolutions involving science (in the sixteenth and seventeenth centuries), agriculture (in the late eighteenth century in Europe) and industry (predominantly the eighteenth and nineteenth centuries)? The American sociologist Daniel Bell has pointed out, for example, that around a hundred years ago there was a period of intense and rapid technological innovation and change, including the invention or mass deployment of electricity and light, the motor car and the telegraph/telephone. A visit to Thomas Edison's summer home and laboratory in Fort Myers, Florida – now a museum – is a reminder of the spirit of invention and change at the beginning of the twentieth century. Not only was Florida itself opened up for the first time by the railway, but Edison was revolutionizing the world with, among other things, batteries, phonographs, light bulbs and electricity generators. His great friend and neighbour Henry Ford was also doing his bit at that time to change the face of travel.

But valid though this argument is, to some extent it misses the point – the fact that rapid change has happened before in history does not diminish its impact or significance now. Those revolutions caused significant change and sometimes over a relatively short period of time.

It is my belief that this one will too but to assess the potential impact we do need to understand the social context of any technological innovation. In particular, there is the question of what technology might mean for the 'relationships' that companies have with the world, with society. It is this aspect that I want to concentrate on in this chapter rather than general technology predictions, because it has, I believe, important implications for how businesses conduct themselves.

In any case, other authors have already given excellent accounts of technological prospects and the broader implications of the infamous laws of Moore and Metcalfe.[6] Briefly, to remind readers – if any need doing so – Moore's Law states that processing power doubles every 18 months.[7] This means that computer speeds will continue to increase at an ever-faster rate, while costs reduce too. In the context of this book, this is not that important except that computer chips, and hence computer intelligence, will be embedded in more and more 'appliances'. More important for my overall argument is Metcalfe's Law for the social and commercial implications that I outline below (and consider again in Chapter 10). Again briefly, Metcalfe's Law focuses on the fact that the power (or value) of a network increases disproportionately to the number of connected users. Although it is usually presented as 'the value of a network rises at a rate equal to the square of the numbers using it' this is, in reality, an approximation.[8] The important thing about Metcalfe's Law is that it explains not only why the Internet's importance and reach is growing rapidly but also why people are attracted to it. As Stewart Brand notes: 'Metcalfe's Law explains why 50 million people *had* to get on the Internet in just a few years. The aggregate value of other users was so great that they could not afford to miss the boat.'[9]

Because of this, my own view – based on our work at the Future Foundation – is that ubiquitous access to interactive services is now inevitable and could happen quite quickly. In North America, across Europe and in other parts of the developed world we are already witnessing very fast uptake of Internet-based technologies. Much of this Internet access is currently via PCs and the proportion of households connected in this way will continue to grow for a few years yet. But it is not just PCs that will provide interactivity, so too will digital televisions, mobile phones and games consoles. At the Future Foundation, we expect 50 per cent of British homes to have a digital TV by 2002 and, in principle, all of these could have interactive capabilities. Within five years, a substantial majority of the population will have Internet access in some form or other (Figure 6.1).

But potentially the most important development is the new generation of Internet-enabled mobile phones and other portable devices.[10] In European terms, Britain has by no means the highest

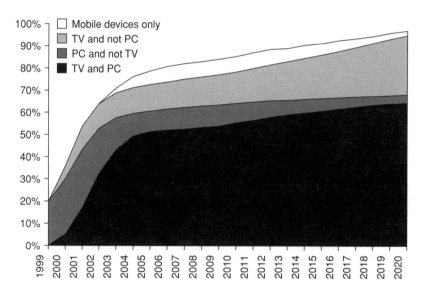

Figure 6.1   Access to interactivity via various platforms. Forecasts for the UK.

Source: *n*Vision/Future Foundation.

penetration rates and usage of mobile phones – the Scandinavian countries hold that honour. But even in Britain, 50 per cent of those who are teenagers or older now own a mobile phone and the Future Foundation estimates that this could be 90 per cent in five years' time. Many of these will be Internet-enabled, allowing people to get news, shop and access information databases when and where they like.

In the less advanced economies the new media environment is, of course, less developed. In Latin America, for example, in 1999 PC penetration was below 10 per cent, while Internet penetration was between 1 and 2 per cent in most countries. This compares with television penetration in these countries of 90 or more per cent. If the Internet becomes as ubiquitous as the television – as it surely will – then this suggests high degrees of penetration eventually across the globe. Unfortunately, the problem in such countries is the lack of fixed telephone lines into people's homes, with between 10 and 20 phones per 100 people in Latin America compared to around 70 per 100 in the United States. A solution may be on hand, though, with mobile telephony which can bypass the need for heavy fixed line infrastructure investment. Already the continent is rapidly embracing mobile technology with the number of mobile phone users growing during the course of 1999 by 83 per cent in Mexico, 66 per cent in Brazil, 34 per cent in Venezuela and 31 per cent in Argentina.

But if we can be reasonably certain that interactive capabilities will exist for the majority of people in the developed world within five or ten years and for the whole world at some time after that, what is less certain is what impact this will have on the way companies do business. There are, though, already some indications of how this might develop. Three aspects – a perception of a faster pace of change, a revolution in time and space and increased 'connections' within an ever more networked society – are leading to a new form and set of relationships for companies to deal with.

A RUNAWAY WORLD

The technological revolution clearly helps to promote the idea that the pace of change in life is getting quicker. The time scales involved in new product launches are now so short that it is hard to know exactly when to buy, as a better product is likely to appear tomorrow. Nowhere is this more true than with computers as they get faster and faster (and cheaper and cheaper) on a regular basis. Whole new technologies appear overnight. The result, according to Anthony Giddens (who is Dean of the London School of Economics), is that it 'feels like a world out of control; a runaway world'.[11] Whether people actually feel less in control of their own lives and less secure as a result of this is uncertain. What we do know is that the desire to be in control is high (Figure 6.2).

But despite the lack of evidence to support or refute the thesis of a 'runaway world', there clearly is something in the idea even if it can sometimes be over-embellished. Things can, and do, change rapidly; people have a wider range of choices; fewer employees have (and, it should be said, want) a job for life. If things are not

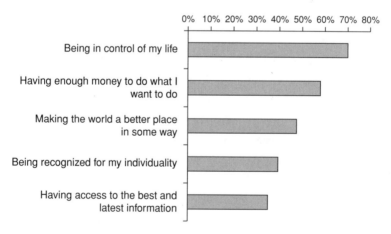

Figure 6.2 Desire to be in control. Proportion rating each element as 'very important' in their lives.

Source: *n*Vision/Future Foundations.

completely uncertain and out of control, they are less certain, less given than in the past.

This creates a seeming paradox in that it promotes the rise of short-termism (you are only as good as last quarter's results) while simultaneously focusing attention on the future (as demonstrated by the plethora of books on futurology). The problem is that if things are moving so fast it becomes all the more important to anticipate change but harder to do so accurately. As Stewart Brand points out in his book *The Clock of the Long Now*:

> If taking thought for the future was essential in steady times, how much more important is it in accelerating times, and how much harder? It becomes both crucial and seemingly impossible.[12]

It is not just IT, but scientific innovation – aided, of course, by technology – that in general is speeding up, affecting people's lives more directly. There are more scientists at work today than in the rest of human history[13] and thanks to information technology they work much more closely together than in the past. This accelerates the process of innovation. As Sir Alec Broers, the vice-chancellor of Cambridge University, noted in his study of the innovation process:

> The innovation matrix extends across groups of researchers and, in many cases, across nations and the world. . . . This is perhaps the area of greatest change [in scientific research] over the last 100 years.[14]

One result of this perception of a quickening pace of change is the development of what I call a *culture of immediacy*. Because people feel the world is moving so fast – because new technology like mobile phones allows them to do it – people increasingly want, and expect, things to happen or be done immediately. For example, in some research conducted by the Future Foundation, people were asked how they would like to order a holiday if they had chosen it one evening, either after watching a television programme or reading a brochure. Respondents were given a variety of options that included going to a travel agent, or

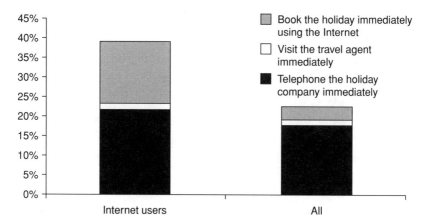

Figure 6.3 A culture of immediacy? Most likely method of ordering a holiday after choosing from a brochure/TV programme etc.

Source: *n*Vision/Future Foundation.

ordering via the telephone or the Internet. They were also asked whether they would do the ordering immediately or would wait until the next day (or later). Even though, in this instance, it does not really matter when it takes place, Figure 6.3 shows that a significant minority – a quarter – would want to order there and then. More importantly, four out of ten Internet users would do so, although many of these would use the telephone rather than the Internet (suggesting that in these initial stages of the Internet there remain some barriers to usage). Access to technology has an impact, it seems, not just on, say, the channels of distribution (the how people order) but on the psychology of it ('I want it now'). Technology enables people to do things more quickly – it allows immediate response.

A NEW CONCEPT OF TIME AND SPACE

So, new technology is influencing how we perceive time. But it is also affecting our sense of space – where we want to, or feel able to do things. This is one of the reasons why the digital revolution is potentially so disruptive. Space and time – the where and when – are critical aspects of not only social and economic life but even of our sense of identity. As sociologist Manuel Castells has noted:

> the new communication system radically transforms space and time, the fundamental dimensions of human life.[15]

Of course, the current phase of technological innovation is not the only one that has impacted on time and space. Railways and cars opened up countries in the last century and electricity opened up the night. More recently, the telephone allowed immediate real-time conversation between places miles apart. The washing machine allowed laundry to come into the home and the television created, in effect, a home cinema. All these inventions affected the when and where, as well as the how. And all of them were hugely successful, to the point that they are now largely ubiquitous, exactly because they transformed time and space.

The importance of this particular revolution in terms of time and space is twofold. First, as I discuss in the next section, it is impacting on communications – both personal and with and between businesses. Second, the new technology is liberating because it is mobile. Think about those previous inventions that I have already mentioned – it is only the motor car that, as an 'appliance', was truly mobile; and look at the importance and success of that. A more recent example was the Sony Walkman, or before that the transistor radio (and look too at the success of those). But the difference this time is that the technology is not only mobile but is potentially interactive too.

People are spending more time on the move – a trend that is likely to be aided and abetted by the new technology. Analysis of time diary data shows that the amount of time the average Briton spends neither at home, nor at work has nearly doubled over the course of the last forty years (Figure 6.4). The reason is

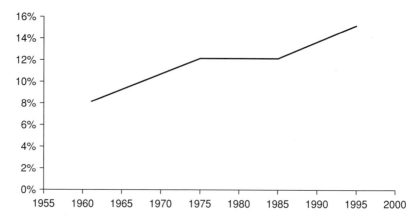

Figure 6.4   Space – the new frontier? Percentage of waking hours spent neither at home nor at work.

Source: Author's analysis of data contained in *Leisure in the UK Across the 20th Century*, Institute for Social and Economic Research.[16]

that we are spending more time on out-and-about activities like going to bars, restaurants and other leisure pursuits and on shopping and non-work travelling (Figure 6.5).

What the new interactive mobile technology will allow is the ability to access information anywhere and communicate with companies in any location. People could look at holidays, and even order one, while having a drink in a bar with friends. They could change their supplier of car insurance after being recommended to another company by a friend who is driving them to a football match. They could choose a restaurant while on a train or watch a sports event while sitting in the park.

So, the technology has the potential to revolutionize *when and where* things are done. Wherever and whenever something is currently done (one's banking, or the purchase of insurance, for example) may in the future be done somewhere else and at a different time. Understanding and anticipating this revolution in space and time will be a critical factor in business success in the future.

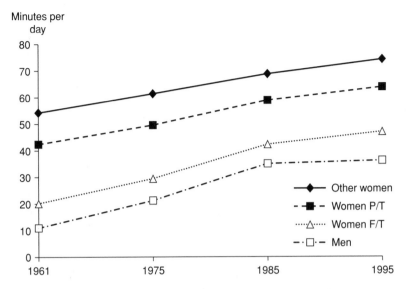

Figure 6.5 Time spent on shopping and domestic travel. Minutes per person per day.

Source: Jonathan Gershuny.[17]

There are two major caveats to make about this, however. First, note from Figure 6.4 that the proportion of time currently spent neither at home nor at work is only 15 per cent of waking hours. Despite the increase in time spent on out of the home leisure and related activities, the largest part of people's lives are still spent in their house or apartment. This suggests to me that a lot of digital entertainment consumption, product information gathering and purchasing will still take place at home. Second, because people have the technological capability of doing something does not mean they will inevitably embrace it. The offer of being able to receive information or carry out a transaction, for instance, in a different place will only be taken up if it offers some benefits to the consumer. It is the interaction between the technology and people and their needs that will define the success of any initiative.

SMALL WORLD, BIG WORLD

Perhaps the most important aspect of the new technology is the transformation it is having on communications, both social and business.

As more people link up to the Internet, as more people have more fixed-line and mobile telephones, so not only are more connections possible, but more 'conversations' in fact take place. Human beings are, after all, social animals and it seems that if we are given tools that aid communication then we will communicate more. Data from Britain show that communications traffic continues to grow (Figure 6.6).

This increased number of connections and the communications that flow from it – be it fixed or mobile phone calls, e-mail, SMS messages, bulletin boards, chat lines or even just accessing web sites – has important implications for business. First, it empowers consumers by providing them with much more information. This ranges from the ability to compare prices (and performance) via the Internet to the increasing importance of word-of-mouth. It is much

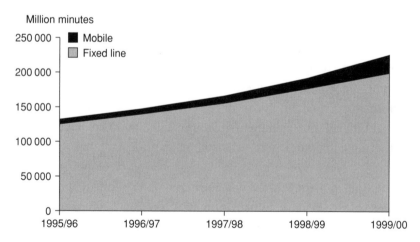

Figure 6.6 Growth in communications traffic. Fixed line phone calls (including Internet) plus mobile calls – minutes.
Source: OFTEL.

easier for one consumer to tell another or a whole group of others that a product is a 'must buy' or a 'must avoid'.

Second, these new communications channels provide advocacy groups an easy outlet for their campaigns. This can vary from the anti-capitalist or anti-advertising 'culture jammers'[18] to the free market fuel price activists who mounted an e-mail campaign against fuel taxes in the United States and Europe in the summer of 2000.

All this not only has some direct impact on how companies need to operate and behave, as I outline below, but it also inherently increases the chances of volatile behaviour as I discuss in a later chapter. More connections and more communications mean good and bad news can travel further and faster than it has ever done before.

RESPONDING TO THE TECHNOLOGICAL REVOLUTION

The implications of this quickening pace of change, the new landscape of time and space and the increase of connectivity and communications are profound.

At a more mundane level, it raises some important operational issues. For instance, as people communicate more via electronic media, so they leave a trail of information about themselves. This might be unbeknown to them, as their web site visits are tracked for example, or even when information is consciously provided on registration or application forms. All this will increase the importance of data protection as a consumer concern. Those companies that abuse the information provided to them by consumers are unlikely to be forgiven, something that a number of proponents of new media marketing sometimes forget. (The so-called 'one-to-one' marketing, for instance, only works if a company has sufficient information about consumers to properly target offers at them.

That information will not be provided to companies with a bad reputation or who are not trusted.) Clearly, being a citizen brand involves taking data protection issues very seriously.

At the same time, the emergence of a culture of immediacy will mean that faster and faster responses will be expected from companies. Businesses need to be operationally organized to be able to respond to consumer requests for information, complaints and orders promptly. The Internet suggests immediate response – companies will need to deliver it.

As important as these points is the more strategic issue of how technology will impact on the relationship between businesses and their customers.

As I have already argued, digital technology empowers consumers by providing them with more choice and reduced barriers to changing brands. It also encourages and enables the customer to have far greater access to a company, allowing the checking of ethical policy for example (although, in reality few consumers are likely to do so on a regular basis). More worryingly, it offers major opportunities for consumer 'terrorism' – for individuals or organizations to mount campaigns against companies or brands they have some complaint or grudge against.

This is where Seely Brown and Duguid's point about understanding the social context of technology becomes important. The new technology is an *equalizer* in the relationship between business and consumer and an *individualizer* – as consumer tastes fragment, so people expect individual offers and treatments. In this environment the social aspects of the exchange (whether the actual exchange itself involves information, money, product or service) becomes more important,[19] as does the role of technology in that. So, to understand the relevance of this, we need to understand more about consumer attitudes to choice, the factors influencing it and the rationality of the behaviour and attitudes to companies, brands and consumer 'terrorism'. This is what I turn to next.

COPING
WITH CHOICE

CHAPTER 7

COPING WITH CHOICE

*T*he trends that I have been discussing in the last two chapters – growing affluence for the many, globalization and the technological revolution – are leading to a number of important developments beyond those I have already outlined. But three – the explosion of choice, a reappraisal of authority and trust and attitudes towards companies – are specially relevant for the way companies themselves operate. The next few chapters are devoted to these themes beginning, in this one, with the issue of choice.

Increased choice for consumers is clearly a relevant matter for companies as it reflects two important trends in markets – one to do with demand, the other with supply – which I have already discussed. In terms of demand, there is clearly a growing fragmentation of tastes as affluence rises, discretionary income increases and consumers become more cosmopolitan in their outlook and confident in their own individual choices. There are fewer economic, social and institutional constraints to what people can and cannot do; fewer peer group or value-based barriers to choice. On the supply side, the inevitable outcome of globalization and deregulation has been more open and competitive markets, often leading to a greater range of goods and services available to consumers. Some have argued that globalization can reduce choice as an ever smaller number of large (multinational) companies push a standardized (and often Americanized) offer into previously diverse markets. While there is something in this argument, in my view the net effect of globalization has been to increase choice. Just look at the range of goods that are available from around the world in British or American or French supermarkets that previously have not been there. As I show later, this is not restricted to supermarkets. In a range of areas, there are more products and services to meet a broader range of consumer tastes and needs than ever before.

But why is increasing consumer choice relevant to the concept of citizen brands? It is because it raises a number of questions that are critical to branding itself. What happens to branding in a world of greater choice? How does a company or product differentiate itself? Is increasing promiscuity inevitable?

I will come back to these questions but first I want to consider the degree of choice and the different areas of people's lives where it is most noticeable.

EXPLOSION OF CHOICE?

I have already mentioned the increased choice in grocery stores and it is perhaps the clearest area where the range of products available to consumers has grown. As local shops have closed in favour of first supermarkets, then superstores and finally hypermarkets, so, inevitably, the array of produce available to people on their regular shopping trips has increased. Some may bemoan the closure of local stores, catering to local needs and with personal-

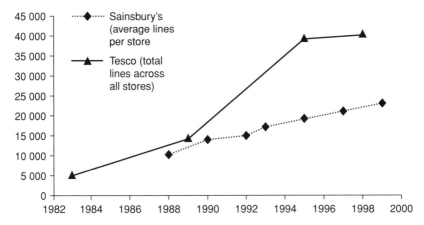

Figure 7.1 Increasing choice in supermarkets. Number of different products available.

Source: IDG Account Management series.

ized service[1] but surely no one can dispute that there is literally more available now. For example, British grocer Tesco had in total 5000 lines across its stores in 1983. By 1998 this figure had increased to 40 000. Another grocer, Sainsbury's, had an average of 10 500 lines in each store in 1988, a figure that had increased to 23 000 by 1999 (Figure 7.1).

In part this is due to goods being available that were just not obtainable before. Exotic fruits and vegetables from around the world are flown in fresh every day. French cheese, Indian spices and Japanese sauces are there to cater for the growing interest in a wider set of multicultural culinary experiences. New, ready-prepared chilled meals are presented to not only whet appetites but to make life easier at the same time. Even for more mundane products the array of choices is bewildering. A large supermarket will carry a huge range of shampoos, conditioners, cooking oils, beers and breakfast cereals. On a recent trip to a local store I found 14 different types of dental floss!

Not only are shops large enough to carry this range and, thanks to globalization, able to offer produce from around the world, but it seems that consumers welcome the choice too. The *individualization* of consumption means that products are not bought for the family, but for individual members within it. This complicates the shopping process, as one middle-aged female shopper noted in some research conducted for British retail bank Abbey National:

> I have to get different sorts of cereal for everyone, different sorts of shampoo, different sorts of coffee.[2]

Consumer research reveals that the average British household now has six different types of cleaning products, three different types of shampoo and three different breakfast cereals, with a general tendency for younger people to have a greater range of these products than older people[3] (Figure 7.2). In part this reflects the fact that people expect to have their own choices in a number of areas, but it also demonstrates how products themselves are moving away from the general purpose to the more specific. There are now different

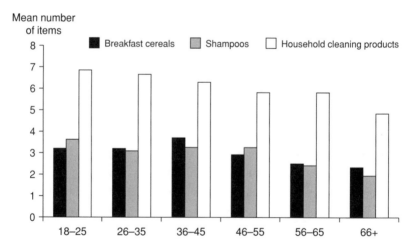

Figure 7.2 Number of different kinds of product in the home. Mean scores by age.

Source: *Complicated Lives*, Abbey National/Future Foundation.

types of hair care products for different occasions. In terms of household cleaning there are different formulations for different purposes:
creams, mousses, wipes and sprays; for use on floors, windows,
bathrooms, toilets, kitchens, ovens (and, of course, in a range of
scents and finishes).

Another interviewee in the Abbey National research – a
woman in her 70s – summed up how much things have changed
over the last fifty-odd years:

> In my day, we just had roast on Sunday, rissoles on Monday, a shep-
> herds pie or something on Tuesday, fish on Fridays – every day you
> knew what you were going to eat. You didn't eat things like chicken
> – that was a luxury, there was less choice.[4]

This is another example of the benefits of prosperity that we
sometimes fail to realize. People now have much more choice
about what to eat, about what to drink and about what personal
care products to use, for example. Of course, they can also choose
to have someone else prepare their food for them. The home
meal replacement market (those chilled, ready to cook prepara-
tions that I referred to earlier) is now worth £200 million in
Britain[5] and is growing rapidly; market research company A. C.
Nielsen expects it to be worth £600 million by 2003. Spending
on meals bought away from home has risen from 11 per cent of
UK food expenditure in 1968 to 24 per cent in 1998. In the
United States, the ready meal/take-away market is currently worth
a staggering £44 billion.[6]

Another example of the impact of a more connoisseur attitude towards food and drink and the implications for choice is
that of the new breed of coffee shops that have sprung up. In a
local one near my office there are a number of different styles of
coffee (ranging from espresso, through macchiato, to latte and
cappuchino), three different types of milk (normal, semi-skimmed
and skimmed), the option of brown or white sugar or sweetener
or none at all and a choice for most styles of three different cup

sizes. When you add in the options for different toppings and flavourings, of decaffeinated or not, and whether you want extra cream there are over 6000 different permutations from which one can choose. If you tried one a day for every day, it would take over sixteen years to try them all. It is no wonder that I need a written note of different colleagues' choices when I do the coffee run – the orders are too varied and too complex to memorize!

But it is not just in grocery or multiple retail stores or even coffee shops that consumers have experienced an explosion of choice. The same has been happening in a range of service sectors too ranging from media to telecommunications to energy suppliers.

Watching television – the activity that we spend so much time on that it dwarfs any other leisure pursuit – is being affected by the explosion of choice. In Britain there are now around 160 channels to choose from if you subscribe to Sky's digital service. Twenty years ago there were only three (Figure 7.3) – choosing which programme to watch has become more complex. The same is happening with other media. There are now nearly 250 commercial radio stations compared to three in 1973 (Figure 7.4).

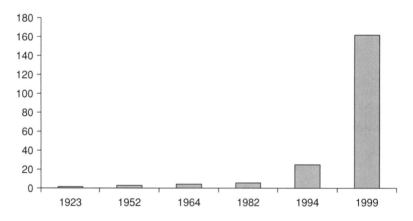

Figure 7.3 Choice of television channels in the UK. Channels available to UK consumers, 1923–1999.

Source: ITC.

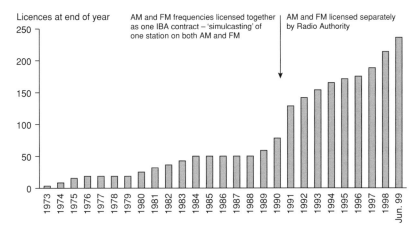

Figure 7.4   Growth in commercial radio stations. Independent local licences on air since launch.

Source: 1974–1990: IBA Archive; 1991–present: Radio Authority.

The number of consumer magazine titles continues to grow. And then there is the new media. With the number of web sites having grown exponentially in recent years it is becoming increasingly difficult to find your way around the world wide web.

Telecommunications is another sector where choice is growing. In Britain there is a choice of at least three suppliers in the fixed-line market and four mobile operators. But, it is in the mobile market when you mix the choice of operator, with the choice of phone manufacturer and then the different payment methods that the decision becomes complex. The different types of tariff offered by the high street phone shop Carphone Warehouse has grown rapidly over the last few years (Figure 7.5).

Privatization in Britain has opened up not only the fixed line telecommunications market to competition and choice but other utility services too. During the 1990s gas and electricity were privatized and under a regime that encouraged competition in the market. The result has been yet more choice for consumers – and some have clearly been quite confused by it.

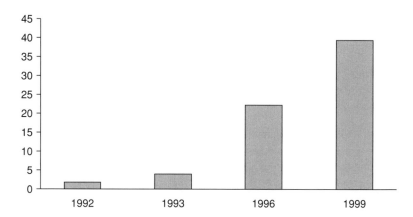

Figure 7.5 Growing complexity in the mobile phone market. Number of different tariffs available from the Carphone Warehouse.

Source: Carphone Warehouse, reported in *Complicated Lives*, Abbey National/ Future Foundation.

Taken together, these government initiatives to provide choice for consumers in the utilities market and to promote rivalry between operators has had a major impact. In 1980, British consumers had no choice at all in the four utility areas of gas, electricity, water and telecommunications. There was just one operator in each. Currently, there are 16 electricity suppliers, 22 companies providing gas, and at least seven telecommunication operators (if you include the mobile companies).[7] As a result of this, whereas consumers had, in 1980, no choice of utility suppliers there are now nearly 2500 permutations across the three areas. And it is likely to get worse. Although currently only large volume water users (those who use over 100 megalitres per year) can choose between different suppliers, the introduction of consumer choice of water supplier is likely within the next few years adding greatly to the permutations across all the utilities. The temptation for some consumers to buy all four services from just one supplier must be strong.

If there is almost too much choice now, technological developments are likely to exacerbate the problem. The Internet allows specialist outlets who cannot justify high street overheads a chance to market to a broader audience without incurring crippling costs. Equally, without the physical constraints of a retail outlet, a much wider range of stock can be offered as Amazon has shown for books and CDs. This is true for exisiting retailers as well as new Internet start-ups like Amazon. British multiple retailer Woolworths carries many more lines in its 'virtual' site on the interactive Open service than even its biggest stores can provide. And then there are the search engines and intelligent 'bots' that can look across the web by category, brand name, product specification and/or price to provide an almost unlimited selection of goods.

DO PEOPLE WANT CHOICE?

This all raises the question of whether consumers really want so much choice. Here, the evidence is far from conclusive. At a broad level, there is no suggestion that people are getting more concerned about the complexity of life in general. For example, research by the Future Foundation[8] shows that the proportion of the population agreeing to the statement 'I don't mind living with the increasing complexity of life' has, at just above 40 per cent, changed little between 1983 and 2000. The only real difference has been a small increase in acceptance for those aged under 35, with around 50 per cent now agreeing with this view. So, if anything, rather than being concerned about living in a more complex world, society is coming to expect it as a fact of life.

But, choice in consumer markets is only one aspect of increasing complexity and it might be one that people are, in fact, less happy about. Equally, the fact that people accept complexity does not mean that they actively enjoy it, nor that they would not welcome help in solving some of the problems it brings. So an acceptance of complexity does not necessarily equate to a desire for the huge expansion of choice that I have outlined above.

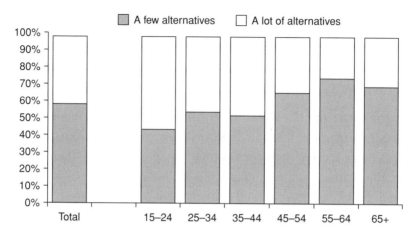

Figure 7.6 Preferred range of choice. In general, when making choices, do you like to have a lot of alternatives or just a few alternatives?
Source: nPower/Future Foundation.

Some research conducted by energy provider nPower[9] suggests there are limits to the amount of choice people want. When asked the broad question 'In general, when making choices, do you like to have a lot of alternatives or just a few alternatives?', nearly six out of ten respondents opted for just a few, with older consumers more likely to say this than younger ones (Figure 7.6).

When asked specifically about the energy sector itself, eight out of ten people said they felt there was a point at which the number of alternatives becomes confusing rather than helpful – most want a limited range to choose from. The difference between what consumers say they want in terms of choice and what they believe to be available certainly suggests an over-abundance of options. When asked to put a figure on the ideal number of energy suppliers to be able to choose from, the average response is six or seven. But consumers believe that the actual number of alternatives available to them is 12. In reality, the choice is even greater with the typical British consumer having some 28 different energy suppliers to select from (Figure 7.7).

Number of suppliers

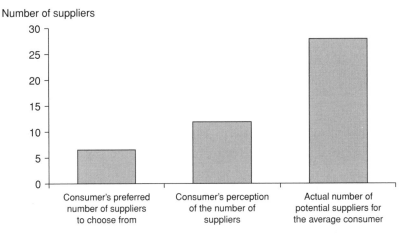

Figure 7.7   Actual, perceived and preferred number of energy suppliers. How many suppliers consumers would prefer to have, how many they think there are and how many there actually are.

Source: nPower/OFGEM/Future Foundation.

This certainly suggests that consumers currently have more choice than they feel they want. Yet against that, I wonder whether people would really be happy to go back to the days when there was less to choose from. In the Abbey National research quoted above, a grandmother described the limited range of clothes available to her:

> In my wardrobe, I had my everyday clothes, skirts, sweaters and blouses, and my Sunday clothes, one coat, two pairs of shoes and a best dress.[10]

In the 1950s she had a small selection of clothes for everyday wear, only two pairs of shoes and one overcoat plus, of course, one smart set of clothes for Sunday. It was quite clear she felt her granddaughter was lucky, and privileged, to have the choice she had. But the granddaughter viewed things differently. For her:

> I have so many clothes, I've got nowhere to put them . . . but I've still got nothing to wear![11]

It is difficult to know how exactly to interpret this statement. Despite having so much, did she still not have enough? Or, was it that she just did not have the right things? But it certainly suggests to me someone who welcomes choice and, indeed, someone who would go out and continue to buy more and more clothes.[12]

From this quick overview of some quantitative and qualitative data and from other research I have done in the area, I draw three conclusions. First, the degree to which consumers welcome choice depends very much on the sector involved and their own individual interests. In an area – energy – that is not particularly exciting and where it is moving from a single public supplier to a multitude of private operators there is little demand for a huge range of choice. In other areas, such as clothes, which are more individualistic and where many people gain real pleasure from the purchasing and consumption process, there can never really be too much choice.

Second, suppliers of goods and services are providing a wider and wider range because it is commercially viable; there is consumer demand for it. People are buying different products and different formulations because they want them. This is, after all, what we would expect with the move towards individualism and the fragmentation of tastes that it implies.

Third, although in some areas people welcome the explosion of choice that has occurred, and even though they might not always explicitly recognize this fact, it clearly does add complexity to their lives – for example, the poor young woman with too many clothes and nothing to wear. This then raises the question of how people are coping with this.

COPING WITH CHOICE

The problem with choice is that it can be not only time-consuming but stressful too. It is not surprising, therefore, that there are a number of different strategies that consumers employ to deal with it. At one extreme, some people clearly use price as a selection tool.

> I shop in the supermarket on Monday, the lady goes around with the machine marking everything down and I walk behind her picking up the bargains.[13]

Where this is the result of poverty, it is not really a strategy for choice – the individual probably does not have much discretion in the first place. But, there is some anecdotal evidence that even those not weighed down by poverty, indeed even some people who are really quite well-off, use price as a selection tool – particularly in areas where they have little intrinsic interest. But beyond price, Figure 7.8 shows the other major options open to people faced with the problem of choice.

The first strategy – and again this applies particularly to those areas of least interest – is to relax the search and selection criteria

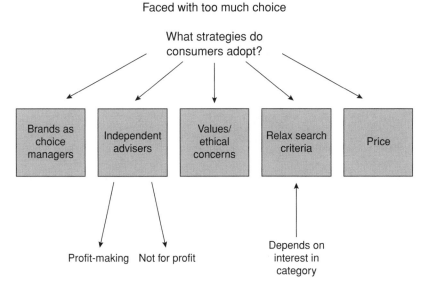

Figure 7.8 Strategies for coping with choice. Schematic representation. Source: Michael Willmott.

in the choice process. In a way, using price is one variation of this, certainly when buying the cheapest and ignoring other questions like performance or value for money. Or, at the opposite end of the scale, and for those who can afford to act like this, price might be effectively ignored. An example of this would be when people just bought what was most convenient. Another example would be where the more affluent did not worry about reliability as they could always just buy a replacement product. At its most extreme, people may deliberately put themselves in positions where their options are limited, as is the case with one middle-aged man:

> I shop on Friday nights, they've sold out of most things . . . saves me having to decide – I just get what's available.[14]

In markets which are not only uninteresting but where the specific choice is unimportant to the consumer or in areas where there is little product differentiation, shoppers may just buy habitually – the same brand as they always choose. Inertia like this, is what produces much of the loyalty that brand managers mistakenly think of as a deep-rooted attachment to the product. But, because this inertia is driven by habit in undifferentiated, uninteresting markets, loyalty is, in fact, skin deep. So, if the product disappoints in any way, or if it is more convenient to buy another brand, the consumer might easily change. Or it could be just through impulse – a desire for a change. Increased choice is, therefore, one of the reasons why loyalty is decreasing. People have the financial discretion, there is a lot of choice and they just do not really care whether they pick one brand or another.

VALUES, ETHICS AND CHOICE

But three other strategies are perhaps more interesting in the context of this book. The first is where people positively choose a product or service because of the values it, or the company providing it, embodies or conveys. And here, ethical concerns can be particularly important, as I have already argued in previous chapters. The data I presented in Chapter 2 demonstrated that for some people this could be an important issue in the consumer decision-making process. For some, it provides a way to negotiate the problem of too much choice, as one middle-aged woman in the research already mentioned highlighted:

> I only eat organic food – that makes it a bit easier – at least I don't have to think with that ... I used to end up with a trolley piled high with things, now if I just go for organic I buy less.[15]

You can see how this strategy might work in other sectors. People might use the fact that a producer has used organic methods to help them in the hugely fragmented and complex area of wine. (Indeed, 'organic' could be as much a 'brand' to assist choice – see below – as Chardonnay, Sauvignon Blanc, Cabernet or Merlot.) Or, in the area of energy, where in the United Kingdom with its large and confusing degree of choice (as I showed earlier) people might choose a 'green' supplier like Unit(e).

In an era of peace and plenty it seems likely that values-based selection will become more important.

ADVISERS AS CHOICE MANAGERS

But an excess of choice clearly provides opportunities for the direct delegation of the decision process, or aspects of it, to others – to what I like to call 'choice managers'. Independent advisers are one example of this; brands are another. Both open up a whole range of new opportunities for potential suppliers.

Already in some sectors like financial services the independent advice market is growing. Here, people pay – either directly or through commission – for specialist advice on what products and services would best suit their needs. But, this could develop in other areas too. Examples would be holidays (where it does exist in a fashion with travel agents but, to my mind, is currently very poorly executed in most cases), electrical appliances, computing or home décor (where there is already some activity in this area with, apparently, a growth in interior design consultants). There has been much talk recently, as well, of personal shoppers who will buy clothes, ornaments and even Christmas gifts for the (presumably) money rich and (presumably) time poor.

So, despite all the talk of disintermediation, this is why we might in fact see an increase in intermediation – others who help us navigate the plethora of choice we face in the modern world.

These advisers also include the media: magazines, newspapers and television programmes with their own 'named' experts who will recommend this product or that service. And increasingly, of course, new media channels as well. Also, not all of these independent advisers will be commercial. Non-profit consumer organizations with a tradition of helping their subscribers and readers choose the best and safest in a given field should be well placed to take advantage of the explosion of choice. *Consumer Reports* in America, *Que Choisir* in France or *Which?* in Britain all have many years' experience of providing independent consumer advice.

BRANDS AS CHOICE MANAGERS

But in some markets perhaps the most important 'choice manager' for many future consumers will be brands. This may seem a strange assertion given the increasing cynicism towards companies that I discuss later and the decrease in loyalty that I have already alluded to in this chapter. Yet, the fact remains that brands can provide a very efficient shortcut for people who have neither the time nor the energy to devote much effort to choosing products and services. This has always been an important role for brands and is likely to continue to be so just because of the increased complexity of life. Although, as a brand consultancy it is hardly impartial in its views on this, I think Interbrand has got it right when it states that:

> In an overloaded, over-communicated and over-informed world, trusted life-editing and life-simplifying brands will be even more critical.[16]

But it could extend too. Some companies will be able to take on new responsibilities for guiding consumers through the quicksand of choice. This could be the intermediaries I mentioned earlier or retailers, who can either offer guidance across a range of manufacturers or can provide a limited, 'edited' choice. (The idea of edited retailing that first arose in the 1980s remains a successful concept in sectors like clothing.) But service providers can fulfil this choice manager role too ('we'll help you choose the best package for your total financial services needs') as could, of course, manufacturers ('I need a transport solution – I'll go to Ford'; 'I need some new electronics – I'll go back to Sony').

This role of brand as guide and choice manager will be specially important in the new media environment. The prospects for established and new brands in cyberspace are potentially huge – cyber guides and cyber brands to help you through the quagmire of the World Wide Web.

At one level, this suggests a great future for brands. But this has to be countered by the fact that at a general level there is an increasing indifference to companies and brands. They are seen as too powerful and, despite the pleadings of management gurus and the subsequent mission statements of most major companies, too little concerned about their customers. This is one reason why the concept of citizen brands is important. A citizen brand is more likely to be accepted as a choice manager because it embodies a range of values that suggest responsible behaviour and (as I showed in Chapter 2) engenders trust.

Increasing affluence (peace and plenty) and growing access to goods and services (globalization and new technology) have helped to accelerate to an almost endless degree the amount of choice people have in their lives. But this, in turn, creates problems: there just is not the time, nor the inclination, to devote unlimited energy to the process of making choices. So, people have to adopt a range of strategies to cope with this proliferation of consumer products and services. I have argued that there are two main ones: changing the search and selection criteria; and relying on choice managers. For the affluent majority, I believe that value-based selection − that it is a good company, is ethical or is a consumer champion − will be increasingly important. And although there is a range of opportunities in the area of choice managers, it is brands (retailers, manufacturers, specialist advisers) − trusted, reliable brands − that are almost certainly going to be most important.

So in this area of choice, it is citizenship, values and branding that are likely to become more important. And as I noted in the introduction, it is the combination of these three that defines the concept of citizen brands. It seems that too much choice is yet another factor in the development of citizen brands.

SURVIVING
A CULTURE
OF FEAR

CHAPTER 8

SURVIVING A CULTURE OF FEAR

CULEX PIPIENS AND THE NEW YORK CONCERT

On Monday 24 July 2000 tens of thousands of New Yorkers were looking forward to attending a New York Philharmonic concert in Central Park. Little did they know that they were about to be disappointed. The stage was built, the weather was fine and the orchestra was ready to play but, at short notice, the evening concert had to be postponed. It eventually took place two days later on Wednesday.

The reason for the postponement was mosquitoes. Or more correctly, it was not the mosquitoes as such (the species concerned, *Culex pipiens*, is the most common mosquito in New York City during the summer) but what they might be carrying – the deadly West Nile virus. The virus had apparently returned, creating alarm among New Yorkers, as it had done the year before when seven people had died from the disease.

For Mayor Rudolph Giuliani the risk to human health of what Reuters noted was 'the virus that causes potentially deadly brain diseases' was too great. 'We would be pushing the odds if we brought that many people into the park' Giuliani declared. 'The concert brings about 30 or 40 thousand people [in] and Health Commissioner Neal Cohen thought it was advisable to cancel that'.[1] So the concert was postponed, the park shut and the whole of it (all 840 acres (340 ha)) sprayed that evening with pesticide to kill the offending mosquitoes.

It was an easy decision for the mayor to make. Mosquitoes with the virus had just been found in Central Park and in the borough of Staten Island. Indeed, following the 'outbreak' in 1999, testing had been taking place across New York during the Winter and Spring to see whether the virus would survive. These tests had identified West Nile in a number of birds (who carry the virus that can then be transferred to humans by mosquitoes) and in 'overwintering' mosquitoes in a number of city boroughs and suburban counties.

It seems certain that the mayor and his health department were aware of these facts and ready to take immediate action at the first sign of significant danger. (It is commonly accepted that pesticide spraying had occurred too late the year before – after the virus had peaked and was already in natural decline.) The positive identification of mosquitoes in Central Park was all they needed to trigger the quick and firm response. Of course there were potential side effects of spraying in an urban area, not least to some of the non-human habitants of the city. But Mayor Giuliani had to protect the health of his citizens. As the *New York Post* reported[2] Giuliani's line was clear:

> I'm sorry, but if it kills animals, it kills animals... . My job . . . is to help protect human life as much as possible.

Rudolph Giuliani was the person who had introduced zero-tolerance policing to New York – now he was applying the same principles to the insect world.

Not only was this an ideal opportunity for the mayor to demonstrate his dynamic and tough credentials but also one where he could show his compassion and concern for his people's well-being. Politically, therefore, this was almost certainly a good move. But was it a rational decision?

A day or so later, I saw the story about the potentially deadly brain disease on television news in Britain. Since I was about to travel with my family to New York I was naturally concerned about the possible dangers of West Nile-carrying mosquitoes. So I decided to do some research into the subject. In these days of the Internet this was not difficult and within a few minutes I was starting to form a different view of the situation.

The Florida Medical Entomology Laboratory – a specialist unit at the University of Florida – told me some of the history of the West Nile virus. It is closely related to St Louis encephalitis a mosquito-borne virus that has been around in the United States for many years with epidemics occurring in Florida in 1959, 1961, 1962, 1977 and 1990. This was not making me feel any better. After stopping off in New York for a few days, we were flying down to Florida for a month. If West Nile did not get us in New York, perhaps St Louis encephalitis would get us in Florida.

I read on with the history. The first reported epidemics of West Nile were in the 1950s in Israel. Subsequent epidemics occurred in the Rhône delta in France in 1962, 1963 and 1964, South Africa in 1974, 1983 and 1984 and in Romania in 1996 and 1997. I had been in southern France in 1962 as a child and travelled through the Rhône delta but until now I had been blissfully unaware of the epidemic (as too had my parents). And, I'd subsequently been or stayed in the Rhône delta on numerous occasions since. If it was so dangerous why had I not been warned of this before? Why were people not worried about going to South Africa or Romania? Why had my travel agent not warned me about St Louis encephalitis when he knew I was going to Florida? Perhaps it was not as dangerous a disease as it seemed.

Further investigation, including a lot of information made available over the web by the New York City Department of Health[3] and the US government's Centers for Disease Control and Prevention (CDC),[4] revealed more telling statistics. In a medical study in the Queens borough of New York, which had been the centre of the virus outbreak in 1999, tests on a sample of individuals suggested that about 2.5 per cent of the population were infected with the West Nile virus during the epidemic. Of these, around 20 per cent developed mild influenza type symptoms as a result of the infection – that is 0.5 per cent of the population of Queens where the virus was most prevalent. According to Dr Ian Lipkin, director of the emerging diseases laboratory, University of California at Irvine, only around 1 per cent of those infected develop encephalitis, the inflammation of the brain that can be life threatening.[5] Given that in the Queens sample of 677 people only 19 were seropositive, it was not surprising therefore that none had developed encephalitis if the chance was only one in a hundred. If you are unlucky enough to develop encephalitis, the Centers for Disease Control and Prevention estimates the mortality rate to be between 3 per cent to 15 per cent.

So, it turns out that even in a 'hot spot' like Queens (as the CDC described it), the chances of being infected are pretty low (1 in 40), the chances of developing mild flu-like symptoms as a result of an infection even lower (1 in 200) and the chances of developing encephalitis, 'the potentially deadly brain disease' even lower still (perhaps 1 in 4–5000). The likelihood of developing a serious illness or worst of all dying is very small indeed which is why, in New York – a city, including its suburbs, of twelve million people – the number of deaths during the epidemic in 1999 was just seven. To put that into context, for the space of time that the West Nile virus was a threat in New York (two to three months) there would typically be 120 to 150 murders even though the crime rate has come down so dramatically over the last few years.

Furthermore, it turns out that the virus is much more dangerous for the very young (who have yet to develop fully their immune system), the elderly and those with immune deficiencies (for example, people with cancer, HIV or AIDS). Of the seven people who had died in 1999, all were elderly, three were receiving immunosuppressant drug therapy as part of a cancer treatment and a fourth was HIV positive. It seemed like the chance that I, or any of my family, might be in danger from the disease was very small indeed.

More than that, for those outside the high risk groups it might even have some benefits to be bitten by a West Nile-infected mosquito as it helps to develop immunity to subsequent infection. This could prove useful in further travels around the world as the New York City Department of Health suggested on its web site:

> Does past infection with an arbovirus [West Nile Virus] make a person immune? Yes, infection with an arbovirus can provide immunity to that specific virus and perhaps to other related viruses.[6]

Perhaps I had already been infected when as a young child, but with a fully developed immune system, I had travelled through the Rhône delta in the early 1960s?

This all raised the question as to whether spraying had been necessary at all. The pesticides themselves have potentially harmful side effects, not only to the environment and wildlife but to humans too. Pressure groups like the 'No Spray Coalition' argued that more environmental and human health harm was done by spraying than not.

I would not want to dismiss out of hand concerns about West Nile virus. It clearly is a dangerous disease; it did kill seven people in New York in the summer of 1999; it remains a potential killer around the world and does need constant surveillance. But I have some sympathy for the view that widespread pesticide spraying (it continued after Central Park into other parts of New York City and outlying suburbs) was not a rational response. But, at the same time, I accept that Mayor Giuliani faced a difficult choice. He would be attacked for spraying (as it was far from clear that it was necessary) and he would be attacked if he did not spray for not taking sufficient caution. I think most politicians would have taken the same decision as Giuliani. As I said before, it appeared to be a positive, responsive and concerned approach. To have not sprayed would have been politically riskier – Giuliani took the maybe not so rational, but certainly the more precautionary approach.

Why is this relevant to the concept of citizen brands? It may not be immediately obvious but it is, in fact, potentially very important. This is because it raises questions about citizens' trust in institutions, how rational consumers really are and the degree of volatility that might be experienced in consumer markets and political arenas in the future. To explain why, our story comes back across the Atlantic to England.

WELCOME TO THE PRECAUTIONARY PRINCIPLE

In mid-July 2000 a conference took place at the Royal Institution in London, England. Entitled *The Precautionary Principle* its aim was to discuss the seeming increasing nervousness of society about scientific development, innovation and new ways of doing things. The idea of the precautionary principle has been promoted by environmentalists and conservationists in particular and it argues that unless we can prove that something – a new drug, a new scientific procedure, a new invention – is safe, then we should treat that development with extreme caution. Indeed, in its extreme it argues that we should reject any new development until it is proved to be safe. The principle has increasingly been incorporated into international law and is recognized by bodies like the United Nations and the European Commission.[7]

The conference turned into a heated debate between conservationists arguing for the precautionary principle and scientists arguing against it. The difficulty for the scientific side is that, on the whole, science cannot prove that something is safe. What science can do is search for any evidence that something is unsafe – a similar, but subtly different concept.

Over the centuries science has been built on the idea of the 'null hypothesis'. A hypothesis is developed from the starting point that there is no ('null') difference between two groups within a population, two medical procedures or two lifestyle activities, for example. A test is then carried out to assess whether the null hypothesis – that there is no difference – can be rejected. The implication of a rejection of the null hypothesis is that there may, in fact, be a difference between the samples, treatments, behaviours or whatever. For example, the null hypothesis might be that there is no difference in lung cancer rates between those who smoke cigarettes and those who do not. A large-scale test of smokers and non-smokers might then show that the null hypothesis should be rejected because it is unlikely that the observed differences (that more smokers have lung cancer) could have happened by chance. In other words, we have to reject the idea that there is no difference in lung cancer rates between smokers and non-smokers. This is taken to mean that smoking is almost certainly harmful to people's health. As more studies take place repeating this conclusion then it becomes clearer that on the balance of evidence smoking is dangerous.

This is the basis on which science works. The great philosopher of science Karl Popper made this point many years ago when he emphasized that hypotheses cannot be proved, only refuted; if we fail to falsify a hypothesis then it may be accepted cautiously.[8] From this, Popper argued that no scientific theory could therefore be conclusively established. Note, though, that on this basis, we cannot *prove* that something is *not* harmful.

There is a related and important point. These hypotheses, tests and conclusions take place within our current framework of knowledge. That means that we can never be absolutely certain about anything. Our understanding might change and new techniques and procedures might be developed that allow us to look at issues afresh. Then we might discover evidence that leads us to change our opinion. But, at any given point in time, the scientific, rational approach is to say that given our current knowledge and given the evidence this is safe and this is not.

The precautionary principle changes all that because in its extreme version it says we should not develop anything, make any innovations or change anything at all. By definition, any new thing cannot be proved to be completely safe – so nothing new can be allowed to happen. This undermines the whole scientific basis under which things are tested and decisions made. It undermines the fundamental basis of rational thought and replaces it with decisions based on non-rational ideas (certainly in the way that rationality has been defined for the last few hundred-odd years) and even irrational fears.

Two recent British examples demonstrate the point well: genetically modified foods/organisms (GMOs) and mobile phones. In both, there is no clear evidence that they are harmful to consumers – either eating GMOs or from making calls with mobile phones or being near mobile transmission masts. Yet in the case of GMOs, they have been taken off supermarket shelves; in the case of mobile phones a government report[9] has recommended that the phones themselves should be used with caution while the placing of the transmission units should be restricted.

THE NEW FEAR – GENETICALLY MODIFIED FOODS

With GMOs there are some legitimate concerns about possible unintended impacts on the natural world via cross-pollination, for example, of genetically modified organisms with the resident flora or fauna. Against this, there are some very real potential benefits from GMOs like the reduced use of toxic pesticides or the development of new strains of food products that could dramatically help hunger and disease in the third world. The rational, scientific response to this is controlled tests to assess the potential impacts but this is rejected by conservationists who, applying the precautionary principle, have gone to great lengths to stop all trials.[10]

More understandable in my view are concerns about the power that genetic technology might provide to multinational companies. Monsanto, for example, is accused of deliberately developing 'terminator genes' so that farmers have to buy new seeds from the company each year. In this way, it is suggested, Monsanto has, effectively, complete control over the market. Although Monsanto would of course deny this and some people suggest that the company is, in fact 'a good corporate citizen',[11] for a variety of reasons that I discuss in the next chapter there is increasing distrust of multinational companies.

But, what I have trouble understanding or finding sympathy with is the attitude towards currently available genetically modified foods themselves. To repeat, there is *no* evidence that, for example, genetically modified soya is harmful to humans at all. Yet, research by the Future Foundation shows that four out of ten British consumers are 'concerned about eating GMOs' and six out of ten agree that they 'try not to buy foods containing genetically modified ingredients' (Figure 8.1). Around 40 per cent of people who say they are not concerned about consuming GM foods would still not buy them – a clear demonstration of the precautionary principle at work!

It is for this reason that all the major supermarkets withdrew all genetically modified foods or ingredients from their shelves. They had little choice given the strength of consumer opinion. It is little wonder that the British government had to retreat too, eventually taking an extremely cautious (if less than rational) attitude towards GMO field trials.

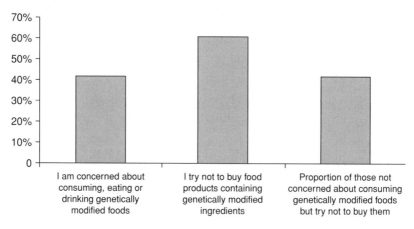

Figure 8.1   Concerns about genetically modified foods. Proportion agreeing.

Source: *n*Vision/Future Foundation.

The most worrying outcome from all this is the impact that it has had on perceptions not so much of science as of scientists. Thus, the Future Foundation's research shows that over the last 20 years there has been no change in the majority view of the benefits of science to progress (see Figure 8.2). Even in the year 2000, in the midst of the genetic engineering furore, the medical potential of that specific technology was acknowledged (Figure 8.3). But, as the chart also shows, many more people agree than disagree that 'you can't trust scientists' in this particular field of science.

We can now see what might be going on in people's minds: 'We hear there is no evidence that GMOs are damaging to your health, but who produces this evidence? Scientists, and we do not trust them. So we do not believe their tests − maybe GMOs do damage your health. Let us be precautionary and not eat genetically modified foods.' Put like this, it seems a rational reaction but ultimately it is not − unless, of course, you believe that the scientists really are not telling the truth.

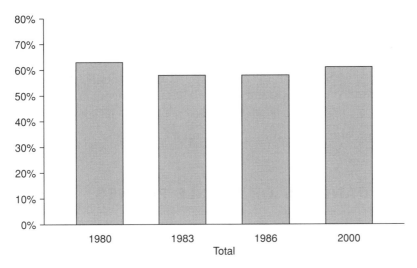

Figure 8.2 Science is still seen as the best hope for progress. Proportion agreeing that 'scientific breakthroughs are our main hope for a better life'.

Source: *n*Vision/Future Foundation.

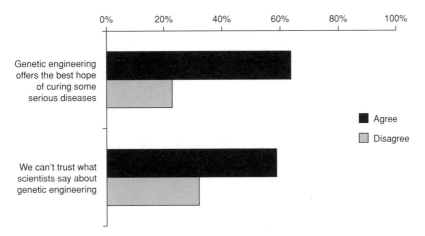

Figure 8.3 Lack of trust in science and genetic engineering. Proportion agreeing/disagreeing with statements – June 2000.

Source: Future Foundation.

Part of the problem here, it seems to me, is not so much scientists but their paymasters. In any discussion of the subject of genetically modified organisms ultimately the issue arises as to who has funded the research. The strong implication is that corporately funded research is not completely independent and objective. It is not so much science that people distrust as scientists who work for large multinational companies. I return to this point later.

THE DANGERS OF MOBILE PHONES

The second example is mobile phones. In May 2000 the British government-backed Stewart Committee reported on its analysis of the potential threats to human health from the use of mobile phones. The committee found no evidence of any harmful effects but recommended that phones and transmission masts should be handled with caution and made a number of recommendations. Here, now, were not environmentalists or individual consumers applying the precautionary principle, but a government-backed committee of experts. The *Financial Times* brilliantly highlighted the potential damage to rational analysis. It is worth quoting most of its leader on the subject:

> There is no evidence that eating strawberries in moderate doses is hazardous. But anti-strawberry lobbyists claim they can cause headaches, loss of memory and cancer. Studies do not support this but they do show interactions with the body's chemistry. On the precautionary principle, therefore, children should not eat strawberries unless absolutely necessary, and never with cream.
>
> Substitute 'mobile telephones', and this gives the general drift of yesterday's report by a committee of experts on the dangers of phoning on the move. Because there is much ignorance about the hazards of radiation, the report's ambivalence will spread unnecessary confusion. The National Radiological Protection Board has said simply that mobile phones are safe. The report criticises the board for insensitivity, but fails to offer good evidence to challenge its conclusion.

Several simple points emerge. First, the radio waves transmitted by mobile telephones have thousands of times less energy than needed to create harmful ionisation effects, such as those of X-rays. Second, the power of radiation from mobiles is too low to raise the temperature of the brain by more than its normal fluctuation. Other forms of damage are speculative.

Third, when telephones are close to a base station they automatically reduce output, perhaps to a thousandth of full power. Fourth, the heating effect of radiation emitted by base stations is 5000 times smaller than that from mobile phones.

It therefore seems perverse to recommend that the erection of base stations should be restricted by tighter planning controls. This change would inhibit competition and require mobiles to transmit at higher power than would otherwise be necessary.

The possibility of danger to children is no more than a possibility, with no firm evidence to support it. Even if proved, it would probably be far less than the danger from eating sweets or going to a disco.

The report makes some sensible, if obvious, conclusions, such as the need for more research, for the monitoring of transmission equipment and for clearer public information. But it has gone over the top in adopting the precautionary principle. This is too often used to justify inchoate fears of the unknown, and should be treated with the greatest caution by scientists. In responding, the government should stick to the facts and apply the strawberry test to everything else.[12]

Quite likely the committee was taking a political view. It has now become too dangerous to give new innovations a completely clean bill of health. By being cautious, you not only are less likely to get a media or pressure group grilling but are also covered if something ever did prove to be wrong. Here, the Stewart Committee was acting in a similar way to Mayor Giuliani in New York.

THE POLITICIZATION OF SCIENCE

Some supporters of the precautionary principle welcome this politicization of science. Brian Wynn, Professor of science studies at Lancaster University and adviser to the British government has argued that political and social concerns should be explicitly considered when assessing scientific evidence.[13] But this is surely exposed for what it is: a means of legitimizing the *rejection* of rational and objective analysis for political gain.

At the Future Foundation we ran an opinion poll just after the Stewart Committee report was published. Not surprisingly, perhaps, we found the precautionary principle had been embraced wholeheartedly by the British public. On the specific issue of mobile phones, nearly three-quarters agreed that 'because of the possible health effects mobile phones should carry a government health warning' with, amazingly, two-thirds of current mobile phone users agreeing. Three-quarters of the respondents also agreed with the more general statement 'the government has a responsi-

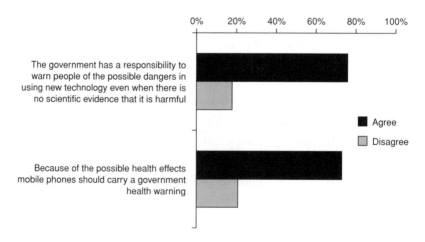

Figure 8.4 Welcome to the precautionary principle. Proportion of the population agreeing that . . .

Source: Future Foundation.

bility to warn people of the possible dangers in using new technology even when there is no scientific evidence that it is harmful' (Figure 8.4). On the face of it, this is a ludicrous suggestion and a potentially costly one for companies too. Every new innovation or technology (why not set-top decoders for digital TV, for example) would have to carry an unspecified health warning.

I'm not saying that GMOs have been proven to be safe or that new GMOs in the future might not pose some threats. We need to remain vigilant and continue objective and rigorous testing. It might possibly be true that at some point in the future mobile phones are proved to be unsafe.

TIME TO SAY GOODBYE TO THE PRECAUTIONARY PRINCIPLE?

But, at this point in time and on the balance of evidence, I am happy to eat genetically modified soya and use my mobile phone (and let my children use it too). A new panic might arise and I might, as I did with the New York West Nile virus, have to research the subject. But my decision on that issue will be based on a balancing of the evidence available. To do otherwise would leave me hostage to irrational fears and concerns – perhaps those dreamt up by others in pursuit of their political goals. It would leave me hostage to a backward-looking, anti-innovation, no-change view of the world. Ultimately, the precautionary principle is a desperately anti-progressive tool since it can be used to argue against *any* new development without the need for any real evidence or proof. As the Social Issues Research Centre warns:

> The narrow philosophy which surrounds the precautionary principle is fundamentally conservative in both political and literal sense.[14]

I agree with Freeman Dyson on this who, in his book *Imagined Worlds*, spells out the dangers of both blinkered, free market enthusiasts (who presumably would reject the idea of citizen brands) and backward-looking conservationists:

> The public dialogue of our era is mainly a debate between free-market economists and conservationists, conservationists trying to preserve the past, free-market economists devaluing the future at a discount rate of seven per cent per year. Neither side of the debate speaks for the future.[15]

The irony, of course, is that the principle could be used against some of its supporters. A report in *Nature Neuroscience*, for example, has suggested that the 'natural' pesticide rotenone that is used in organic farming may have the potential to cause Parkinson's disease.[16] A precautionary principle approach might suggest the banning of organic foods as a result, or the banning of rotenone at least.[17]

Some in the scientific community have, quite rightly in my view, suggested that the precautionary principle be applied to itself. Here, we would say that although we cannot be certain that using the precautionary principle is fundamentally dangerous, the prospect that it is means it should be abandoned immediately. This demonstrates how quite quickly any debate can become completely confused. Both sides could apply the precautionary principle – one side arguing that you cannot prove something is safe, the other that you cannot prove not doing that thing is safe – and with no rational base to arbitrate (as science has provided in the past).

If we go back to the New York West Nile crisis, what was the precautionary course of action? I imagine conservationists would say not to spray but, as I indicated earlier, I suspect Giuliani saw spraying as the precautionary approach. Both could equally and legitimately apply the precautionary principle but what was needed was an objective analysis of the evidence to decide what was best for New York.

Thus, the precautionary principle can be seen for what it is: a political tool to further environmentalist, conservationist and other lobbyists' aims. But the side effects of it: a reduction in faith in science; a rejection of a rational approach to analysing available evidence; and an increase in hysteria and paranoia are ones that are very important for society and companies.

WELCOME TO A CULTURE OF FEAR

The New York incident and the development of the 'precautionary principle' are symptomatic of the rise of what Kent University sociologist Frank Furedi calls the *Culture of Fear*.[18] If one paradox of a world of peace and plenty is the 'burden' of choice that increased affluence enables and the complications this adds to people's lives (as I discussed in the previous chapter) another is people's assessment of risk. It seems that despite being richer and healthier, there are heightened concerns about a range of life issues, be it health, the environment, drugs or crime. Safety, as Furedi points out in his 1997 book on the subject, became 'the fundamental value of the 1990s'. The paradox is that by most measures we live in a safer world.

> Most serious contributors have to accept that in real terms people live longer than before, and that they are more healthy and better off than in previous times.[19]

Furedi notes that in answer to a Gallup question about whether people need to take special care in what they eat (for health reasons) the proportion agreeing doubled between 1947 and 1996. Despite people's health and diet improving, more are worried about what they do eat. This worry about our health is also demonstrated by data that show that the proportion of people in Britain self-reporting longstanding illnesses increased from 21 per cent in 1972 to 35 per cent in 1996.[20]

People are more concerned about their children too. The age at which people let their children play in the street or walk to

Age allowed to . . .

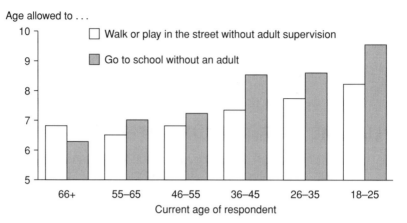

Figure 8.5 Worries about children. Age at which respondent was allowed to . . .

Source: *Complicated Lives*, Abbey National/Future Foundation.

school has increased considerably as parents have worried more and more about the potential dangers facing children (Figure 8.5). But it is far from clear that the streets are any more dangerous now than they were in the past.

Over the last five years crime rates have fallen significantly in Britain as Figure 8.6 shows. Certainly, criminal activity is still high by historical standards, but this quite dramatic reduction has not been mirrored in the public's perception of crime with two-thirds of the population in 2000 believing the crime rate was increasing.[21] Presumably spurred on by politicians and the media the proportion believing this had actually increased since 1998.

American sociologist Barry Glassner published a book two years after Frank Furedi also called *The Culture of Fear*.[22] In it he charts exactly the same paradox in the USA – an objective and measurable improvement in many aspects of people's lives alongside an increase in concerns, fears and hysteria – the same predominant pathology that Furedi identifies in Britain.

Why are so many fears in the air, and so many of them unfounded? Why, as crime rates plunged throughout the 1990s, did two-thirds

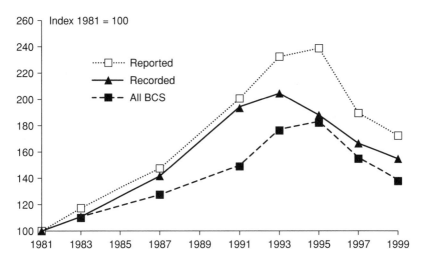

Figure 8.6 Crime rates in Britain. Index of crimes reported to, and recorded by, the police and those identified by victims in the British Crime Survey.

Source: British Crime Survey, Home Office.

of Americans think they were soaring? How did it come about that by mid-decade 62 per cent of us described ourselves as 'truly desperate' about crime – almost twice as many as in the late 1980s, when crime rates were higher? . . .

In the late 1990s the number of drug users had decreased by half compared to a decade earlier; almost two-thirds of high school seniors had never used any illegal drugs, even marijuana. So why did a majority of adults rank drug abuse as the greatest danger to America's youth? Why did nine out of ten believe the drug problem is out of control, and only one in six believe the country was making progress?

Give us a happy ending and we write a new disaster story.[23]

Barry Glassner goes through a long list of scares ranging from road rage to ritual child abuse to violence in the workplace and demonstrates that there is little real evidence to support any of them.

Glassner argues that three forces are stoking up people's irrational hysteria: politicians who win elections by heightening fears; advocacy groups that improve their fund raising capabilities by exaggerating concerns; and the media, conscious that fear and scaremongering sells. Although he doesn't initially include them in the list Glassner does later identify companies as a further agent of the culture of fear. He quotes an example of a hospital in New York that at the height of a scare about child psychiatric problems ran a TV advert that showed a teenage girl with a gun at her head: 'As the screen cut to the hospital's name and phone number, a gunshot rang out and parents were urged to call if they worried about their own children.'

In a different way, a report from a British mutual retailer the Co-op provides another example. Its *Food Crimes*[24] report accused big business of committing seven crimes: blackmail ('the insidious targeting of the public by global big business'), contamination, grievous bodily harm, vandalism, cannibalism, pillage ('the careless exploitation of countries') and fraud. While the Co-op was operating from the highest of principles – it really does want to improve food and animal welfare standards – and had no specific desire to increase a culture of fear, the effect was to increase concern about a range of issues and the behaviour of multinational companies specifically.

And, as the *New York Times* put it in an article on 30 July 2000, an environment of scare and hysteria provides ample opportunities for making a noise. The article entitled 'The Things People Choose to Fear' was prompted by the West Nile crisis and finished with the following tale:

> And some players just want a piece of the action. Howard Rubenstein Associates, for example, the big New York public relations firm better known for representing high-gloss celebrities, began calling reporters last week with a whispered tip about a new turn in the virus story: a mosquito, infected with West Nile, that apparently feeds during the day, had just been discovered by researchers at Fordham University. The researchers themselves were a bit more circumspect; they are not quite sure yet how common their new mosquito, *Aedes japonicus*, is, how well it transmits the virus, or whether it even bites people.[25]

Both Furedi's and Glassner's books are a rallying call for a return to rationality (as is the argument against the precautionary principle) but I wonder whether this will happen. As Stuart Sutherland showed in his book *Irrationality: The Enemy Within*,[26] we are already a pretty irrational society. How else can one explain the changes that people make to their behaviour as a result of very low, or effectively zero, risk exposure (many food, health and crime scares, for example) and the increase in participation in high risk areas like dangerous sports? And the combined force of politicians, campaigners and the media is likely to mean we are going to stay that way or even get worse.

In defence of people's attitude to risk it is clear that an important issue is the perceived control that people have over any activity or event and the choices that are available to them. So, driving in cars is more dangerous than travelling by plane or train, yet the driver feels ultimately in control of events. With BSE or genetically modified foods, part of the problem was not having a choice – not knowing whether a food product contained genetically modified soya or whether the beef you were eating was from an infected herd. It is only when they have this choice and this control that people may then weigh up the benefits that accrue from an activity against the risk. They will use a mobile phone even though they believe it is dangerous or go skiing in the knowledge that it is a dangerous sport.

CULTURE OF FEAR AND CITIZEN BRANDS

Why is the phenomenon of a 'culture of fear' important to the idea of citizen brands? It is so for three reasons. First, a climate of fear tends to reduce trust in a range of institutions. If there are scares, claims and counter-claims it is difficult to know who to believe and who to trust. Worryingly, companies seem to fare particularly badly on this count. Second, with the potential volatility in markets that scares imply, it is much harder for companies to plan, and the potential disruption could be great. Take the mobile phone example. Some of the most successful and currently highly valued companies in the world like Nokia or Vodafone could be devastated if the scare about mobile phones turned into full-blown panic.

Third, companies must get away from the idea that consumers necessarily act as rational beings – fed as they are by misinformation from a variety of sources. Of course, rationality is not always in a company's interest and, dare I say it, it might suit a company in the short-term to play on the back of irrational hysteria (as the hospital example showed).

Ultimately, though, the culture of fear is not good news for companies. Consumers are less likely to trust companies generally, less likely to analyse objectively information about companies and more likely to over-react to scare stories.

But, being a citizen brand might be one way to smooth out the ups and downs inherent in a culture of fear. Being an open and transparent organization, that offers real choice and full information to consumers, that is trusted, has a reputation for honesty and a bank of goodwill is a defensive manoeuvre that will be increasingly important for companies to follow.

SO-SO LOGO

CHAPTER 9

SO-SO LOGO

The Increasing Cynicism
of Consumers

*I*n *No Logo*, Naomi Klein produced one of the most significant business books of 2000. Its importance lies in the fact that she identified and articulated a disturbing trend for companies – an increase in cynicism about businesses, and multinationals in particular, and the way they operate in the global economy. Although, as I discuss later I believe some of her analysis is misguided, the book's huge success reflects the fact that it clearly touched a nerve – there was something in it that mirrored people's own view of the world; their fears and concerns.

Well written and beautifully presented, the book is a seriously researched critique of global companies and their brands. Much of Klein's analysis is sound and, as I show later, some of my own research supports the central thesis that consumers are becoming more wary of business, its motives and its practices. But the tone is nothing less than revolutionary. Klein believes that corporations and their marketing and branding strategies have only themselves to blame:

> By attempting to enclose our shared culture in sanitized and controlled brand cocoons, these corporations have themselves created the surge of opposition described in this book. By thirstily absorbing social critiques and political movements as sources of brand 'meaning', they have radicalized that opposition still further. By abandoning their traditional role as direct, secure employers to pursue their branding dreams, they have lost the loyalty that once protected them from citizen rage.[1]

Klein overtly sympathizes with activist organizations like Reclaim the Streets and expects citizens and consumers to rise up in protest:

> a different agenda has taken hold, one that embraces globalization but seeks to wrest it from the grasp of the multinationals. Ethical shareholders, culture jammers, street reclaimers, McUnion organizers, human-rights activists, school-logo fighters and Internet corporate watchdogs are at the early stages of demanding a citizen-centered alternative to the international rule of brands. That demand . . . is to build a resistance . . . that is as global, and as capable of co-ordinated action, as the multinational corporations that it seeks to subvert.[2]

This is heady stuff, and together with the trendy catchphrases – 'brand bombing', 'cool hunters', 'oppression nostalgia', 'market marsala', are just some examples – explains, in part, the attraction of the book to many readers.

BRANDS, GOVERNMENT AND GLOBALIZATION

Naomi Klein is not alone in her criticism of the role of business and its insidious involvement in everyday life. British journalist George Monbiot's book *Captive State*[3] is another attack on modern capitalism. Monbiot's main anger, however, is directed at the governments – both national and local – that are pandering to corporate demands. He rails against the way public authorities have allowed themselves (he argues) to be corrupted by big business, effectively ceding power to them. As such, Monbiot does not spend much time on businesses themselves apart from the odd occasion when he picks out particular villains (as when he intriguingly claims that grocery retailer Tesco is 'widely blamed for shattering communities'). But the major emphasis is on the democratically elected bodies that embrace the anti-democratic ways of big business. Ultimately, though, the conclusion is the same as Naomi Klein's but if anything even more cataclysmic:

> The struggle between people and corporations will be the defining battle of the twenty-first century. If the corporations win, liberal democracy will come to an end.[4]

Both authors fundamentally believe that globalization is bad. They are particularly concerned about the loss of manufacturing jobs in developed economies and the exploitation of workers in the developing world. But this can be questioned in two ways. First, can globalization be stopped? Second, is it, in fact, bad for the rich, developed world to export jobs to the third world? I must say that on both points I tend to agree with the more pragmatic views of Claire Short (a renowned left-winger) who as International Development Secretary in Tony Blair's government made the point that:

> Globalisation is a set of economic and technological developments in the world which are a fact of history. The job is to manage history not to oppose it.[5]

She went on to highlight the idealistic view that some have of third world life, suggesting that there was:

> 'a small but dangerous' group of people who romanticise poverty in developing countries and hold a visceral opposition to the mere idea of economic development.[6]

Another pragmatist about globalization is United Nations secretary general Kofi Annan. In a speech to the Davos World Economic Forum in 1999 he said:

> It would be tragic if local or national communities react to the challenge and shortcomings of globalisation by repeating the mistakes of history, and turning in on themselves. Why? Because open markets offer the only realistic hope of pulling people in developing countries out of abject poverty, while sustaining prosperity in the industrialised world.[7]

DECLINING FAITH IN COMPANIES

It would be easy to dismiss the views of writers like Klein and Monbiot as the rants of old-style anti-capitalists who have modernized their analysis, tone and presentation but not, in fact, their underlying beliefs. Certainly, it is true that Klein, almost inevitably, is dismissive of new 'third-way' politics. New Labour is apparently 'right-of-centre' and an insult to its name:

> Blair . . . changed the name of his party from an actual description of its loyalties and policy proclivities (that would be 'labour') to the brand-asset descriptor 'New Labour'. His is not the Labour Party but a labor-scented party.[8]

But to dismiss these two out of hand would miss the point. Klein and Monbiot are clearly expressing, if in extreme form, a populist view. For, throughout the developed world (and in other parts too) citizens are becoming increasingly concerned about the power and veracity of companies. A recent Harris poll in *Business Week*[9] found generally negative views about America's corporations. Two-thirds of respondents agreed that 'having large profits was more important to big business than developing safe, reliable, quality products for consumers', while only a quarter felt that business was excellent or pretty good in 'being straightforward and honest in their dealings with consumers and employees'. Echoing my point in previous chapters about excessive executive pay, three-quarters believe that the top officers of large US companies get paid too much. Large brand-name companies are seen as 'squeezing out local business' and 'reducing local variety and culture' (87 per cent and 75 per cent agreeing respectively), although they are seen as offering more consistent quality and lower prices than local businesses. Most worryingly for the corporate sector, there is a perception of an increasing dislocation between the interests of business and society generally. Figure 9.1 shows that the proportion of US citizens agreeing that 'what is good for business is good for most Americans' declined significantly in the late 1990s. It seems there is little evidence to date of businesses following my suggestion in Chapter 1 that they should put society at the heart of the company.

A similar picture of a decreasing degree of faith in companies is found in Britain. Research by the Future Foundation shows that the proportion of the general public who agree that most companies are fair to consumers has declined over the last twenty years while those who actively disagree has increased (Figure 9.2).

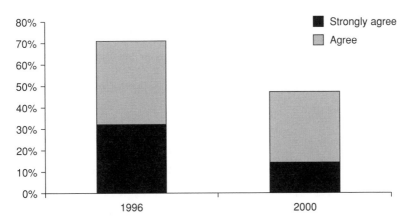

Figure 9.1 Business losing touch with society? Proportion agreeing that 'In general, what is good for business is good for most Americans'.
Source: *Business Week*/Harris.

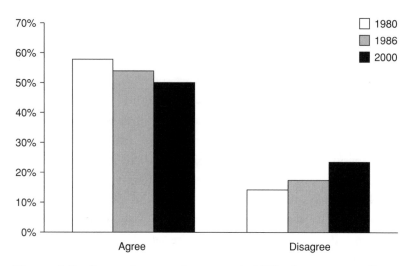

Figure 9.2 Decreasing trust in companies? Whether agree or disagree that most companies are fair to consumers.

Source: *n*Vision/Future Foundation.

British social and market research company MORI has noted the same trend. Since the mid-1970s the proportion agreeing that 'the profits of large British companies help make things better for everyone who buys their products and services' has declined steadily, falling from around 50 per cent in the 1970s to less than half of that in 1999 (Figure 9.3).

None of these on their own are ideal measures of consumer cynicism but together they provide powerful evidence that over time, and on both sides of the Atlantic, consumers are indeed having fundamental doubts about the way companies are operating. This is supported by more research carried out by the Future Foundation in 2000.[10] When asked a range of questions about the globalization process and the behaviour of multinational companies the response is not very positive. Nearly half of consumers agree that 'you can't trust large multinational companies nowadays' with only one in five disagreeing[11] (see Figure 9.5 later). Only around a quarter agree that 'overall global capitalism benefits all' while

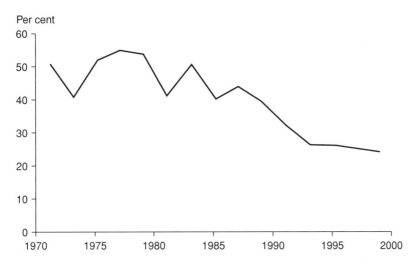

Figure 9.3 Cynicism about business in the UK. Proportion agreeing that the profits of large British companies help make things better for everyone who buys their products and services.

Source: MORI.

nearly four out of ten disagree. And, when asked directly about the amount of power that multinationals have, seven out of ten believe that they 'have too much power and should be stopped now' or that they 'need to be policed and controlled more than they are at present' (18 per cent and 52 per cent respectively – see also Figure 9.4). Clearly, there is a good deal of unease about the role, power and actions of multinational companies in the global economy.

WHY IS IT HAPPENING?

So, if consumers are indeed losing faith and confidence in companies why is this happening? The reasons can be found in some of the previous chapters.

In a world of 'peace and plenty' where many of our traditional sources of fear and loathing have disappeared, it appears that new ones are required to take their place. Add in the unstoppable force of globalization and who now is most powerful; who most threatening? Enter multinational companies – the new villains, the new bogeymen of our times.

Part of the problem, arguably, is the shear size of these corporations. Many multinationals now have a turnover that exceeds those of some countries themselves. Of the world's hundred largest economies, fifty are corporations, while the turnover of the ten biggest businesses is more than the total of that of the world's hundred smallest countries. Shell owns 400 million acres of land, making it larger than 146 countries. The largest 500 companies in the world – many of which are American – are now responsible for over 40 per cent of global wealth and control two-thirds of global trade. Fewer than ten transnational corporations control virtually every aspect of the worldwide food chain.[12]

Inevitably, this raises some questions. If companies are so powerful do we not need to worry about the mechanism for controlling them? As Charles Handy has noted: 'when corporations are bigger than nation states you have to ask who governs them, and for whom.'[13] Anthony Giddens (Dean of the London School of Economics) has made the same point:

> I think for better or for worse you do have to see this as a business civilisation. Most of us did not see the degree to which it would become a business civilisation, because I think certainly a lot of people in the centre and on the left underestimated the power and the significance of markets. In this world, the corporations do have a central role to play, alongside government, and they are, if you like, a kind of secondary invisible global government.[14]

Invisible? Government? No wonder citizens are worried.

WHO HATES COMPANIES?

But, who is most worried about this development. Here, the evidence, certainly from Britain, seems to go against Naomi Klein's supposition that it is young people who are leading the anti-capitalist crusade.

For example, only just over half of 16–24 year olds think global corporations need to be controlled or stopped compared to nearly three-quarters of other adults (Figure 9.4).

I carried out an analysis of this question and the others about multinationals to see what individual characteristic – age, social grade, income, for example – was most associated with different responses. Age emerged as the most important factor in explaining difference with the young being the least likely to hold anti-corporate views. To make the point, another example, Figure 9.5,

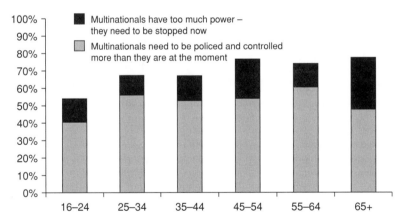

Figure 9.4 Do multinationals have too much power? Some people say that multinationals are too powerful nowadays – which one of these statements comes closest to your own view? (Other statements offered were: 'Multinational companies are ultimately for the good – we need to encourage their continued growth' and 'The power of multinational companies is at about the right level – they should be left to themselves'.)

Source: *n*Vision/Future Foundation.

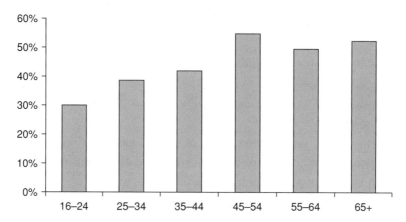

Figure 9.5 Many do not trust multinationals. Proportion agreeing that 'You can't trust multinational companies nowadays'.

Source: *n*Vision/Future Foundation.

shows that twice as many 45–54 year olds agree that you cannot trust multinationals as do 16–24 year olds.

In order to understand these issues better, I carried out a cluster analysis of the data – a statistical technique that groups people together on the basis of their responses to different questions. The results suggest that there are five different groups of consumers based mainly on two issues: whether globalization is seen as a good development or not;[15] and whether multinationals are seen in a generally positive or negative light.[16] The different segments are illustrated in Figure 9.6. One group is pro globalization and pro global corporations (top right-hand quadrant of the figure) while another is pro globalization but more ambivalent about companies. Both groups have a higher incidence of under 35s, and under 25s in particular, in them. There are three segments that are less happy with globalization. The first, in the lower right-hand section of the figure, contains people who are generally rather positive about multinationals but the other two might be described as the core anti-globalization, anti-multinational brigade. Together they represent a bit over a third of the population. They split, however, into two distinct groups – those that are prepared to 'demonstrate if a

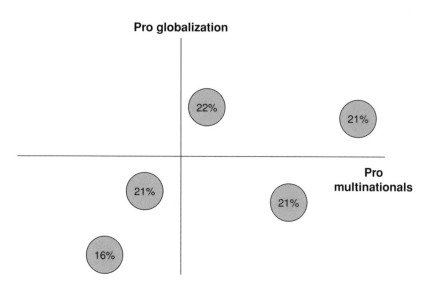

Figure 9.6 Globalization and multinationals – clusters of opinion. Representation of different segments of the population based on responses to a range of attitude questions.

Source: *n*Vision/Future Foundation.

large multinational company had done something wrong' and those that are not. The radical activists – those that say they are happy to demonstrate – represent around one in six of the population. Importantly, the 16–24 year old age group are underrepresented in both these segments. Interestingly, those aged 16–24 who are contained in that radical, protesting, activist group represent just 1 per cent of the population and 10 per cent of 16–24 year olds. It is from this group that protesters at World Trade Organisation and other similar meetings presumably come and from whom organizations like Reclaim the Streets gain their members. They may be highly vocal, visible and disruptive, but they currently represent only a small minority of young people.

This analysis shows that, if anything it is the sixties generation – those who were born in the 1950s and the 1960s – who are the most cynical about global corporations and the youth of today who are least so. Why should this be?

I believe there are two plausible explanations. First, the radicalism of the sixties generation clearly lives on. Research at the Future Foundation shows that this generational cohort is carrying through all of its liberal attitudes and anti-establishment inclinations as it gets older. But, with the onset of 'peace and plenty' and many of the 'battles' for individual freedom of action and expression won, there seems less need for subsequent generations to 'revolt' in a similar way.

Second because of the increases in choice (see Chapter 7) and the development of consumption-based individualism, new entrants into markets – that is the young – find brands, and international ones specially, a very useful mechanism for negotiating their way through the morass of complexity that life now offers. More than that, consumption and the purchase of brands can be an important part of self-identity. As Laura Oswald puts it: 'The subject of consumption is nothing if not an actor in search of an identity'.[17] Wendy Gordon and Ginny Valentine make the same point:

> The 21st century consumer is post-modern to the core. She shifts identities and uses a vast wardrobe of brands to create herself into whoever she wants to be.[18]

My own view is that this is particularly true of younger consumers. But, as they get more experience in the consumption process they become more confident – they still use brands but, if you like, in a more cynical way. So, people grow into their concern about multinational companies and their behaviour – questioning companies is part of becoming middle-aged. This is different from the ideologically-based anti-capitalism of the sixties generation. The small group of young anti-capitalist agitators aside, protest has become less of a generational phenomenon and more of a life stage one.

Interestingly, this progression from youthful acceptance of, and indeed need for, brands followed by a growing cynicism matches Klein's account of her own life experience.

SURVIVING THE CYNICAL CONSUMER

So, to recap on the analysis in this chapter, we see that consumers are becoming more concerned about the behaviour of companies, and multinationals in particular, and more cynical about their intentions. But it is not so much young people as the middle-aged and older consumers who most exhibit these attributes.

There is not much evidence of a large-scale anti-capitalist movement as such but rather an increasing readiness on the part of consumers to expect more of companies (as I have shown earlier in this book) and a willingness to punish them if they do not. This manifests itself in the unsurprisingly much higher proportion of consumers who would boycott a company rather than demonstrate against it (Figure 9.7). I am not saying people will not demonstrate over political, economic or social issues but, if they do, it is more likely to be on a single issue basis rather than a revolt against the system as such. The result is likely to be more

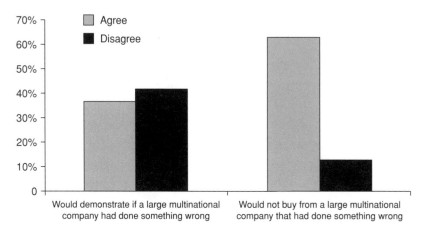

Figure 9.7 Consumer terrorism. Whether would boycott or demonstrate against a multinational that had done something wrong.

Source: *n*Vision/Future Foundation.

of a roller-coaster ride for companies with more brand volatility as consumer cynicism increases and loyalty declines. (Governments might see the same too, as I discuss in the next chapter.) It will not be so much 'no brands' as an ever-changing pastiche of brands as people switch in and switch out on the basis of ethical or other concerns.

There is another issue too – consumers need brands, either as 'choice managers' (see Chapter 7) or as a source of identity. Put simply, brands are too useful for consumers to give them up. This is particularly true of younger people.

No Logo is an influential book and makes some very important points, not least the dangers facing poorly run, exploitative and irresponsible companies. But, at the moment it seems unlikely that we are entering an anti-capitalist, anti-branding world. Rather, what seems more likely to emerge is an era where consumers are ever more critical of companies and increasingly happy to change loyalties.

The solution for business is to be more in touch with society, to develop more responsible marketing and employment policies and, importantly, to be more open and transparent. It is here that some of the cynicism can be countered. Companies and brands will survive in the twenty-first century, but the winners will be citizen brands.

BUTTERFLY
CONSUMERS

CHAPTER 10

BUTTERFLY CONSUMERS

A fter winning the British general election in May 1997, the Labour Party maintained a significant lead over its rivals, the Conservatives, for the next three years. Nothing, it seemed, could stop Labour being re-elected for a second term at the next election expected in 2001. That was until September 2000 when its poll ratings suddenly took a dive. A dispute about the price and high rate of taxation on fuel brought Britain to a halt. Farmers and road hauliers blockaded oil refineries stopping fuel being distributed and within a week, 90 per cent of filling stations had run dry, hospital medical procedures were being postponed and businesses were warning that they would imminently have to shut down operations until fuel supplies resumed.

The protest had begun with an Internet e-mail chain letter campaign in June following a similar movement in the United States. Soon after, the press picked it up and the populist tabloid the *Sun* ran a campaign calling for people not to visit petrol stations on the first day of each month, starting on 1 August. On the day, though, little happened with few people actually participating in the 'boycott the pump' protest. It seemed to have died.

But in September, French lorry drivers and farmers (renowned for their readiness to take direct action) started blockades in France. Within a week, the French government had conceded to some of their demands and the dissent began spreading to other countries across Europe. Spurred on by the success of the French protesters the campaign on fuel prices (and tax especially) was re-ignited in Britain, organized by a loose network of farmers and truckers who coordinated their actions via mobile phones, CB radios and in-cab fax machines. Within a week the nation was on the brink of serious collapse of vital services.

Suddenly, the protest stopped as quickly as it had started – the campaigners recognized that public support was beginning to waver in the light of the severity of the protest's effects. But by then, the impact on the government's popularity had been dramatic.

From around 50 per cent support throughout 2000, in a week this had dropped to the mid-30s (Figure 10.1). This was, in the history of voting intentions, unique as Britain's best-known psephologist David Butler noted:

> Two weeks ago, national opinion polls were indicating, on average, a 15 per cent Labour lead. Today, they put the Conservatives 4 per cent ahead. This is the sharpest change ever recorded.[1]

After that, Labour slowly recovered its position but it had learnt its lesson: another crisis could happen at any time, seemingly out of nothing, and threaten its political prospects. It understood that voters are more volatile now than they ever have been.

The same is true of consumers and consumer markets. Consider the points I have made about different aspects of attitude and behaviour in the second half of this book. I have argued

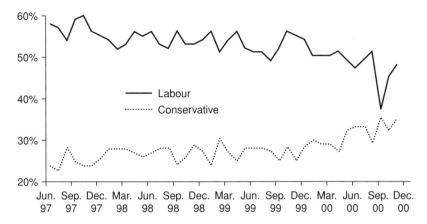

Figure 10.1 The collapse and recovery of Labour support. Likely voting intention.

Source: MORI.

that when consuming – that is when choosing or purchasing products and services – people have:

- more discretion
- a greater number of 'connections'
- a wider range of choice
- less institutional 'direction'
- increasingly irrational concerns and fears
- and greater cynicism towards those providing the goods and services.

Little wonder then that consumer behaviour appears – and, indeed, I would argue is – more volatile. Little wonder that voting behaviour is too. One of the great philosophical and mathematical advances of recent years has been the development of chaos theory. Everyone is aware of the apocryphal example of a butterfly beating its wings in China and causing a storm on the other side of the world. But now we have the prospect of a similar process at work in consumer and political attitudes and behaviour – the development of what one might call 'butterfly consumers'.[2]

WELCOME TO ANARCHY

This is scary stuff, and particularly for large multinational companies. From seemingly nowhere, and fast, tastes can change, brand attractiveness can wane, company profits can soar or plummet. The increasing economic discretion and confidence of consumers added to the communications power of new technology makes for a potent and explosive mix. This is consumer anarchy as sociologist Manuel Castells notes:

> The network society restores some level of power and initiative to individuals and networks of individuals through movements of information. In that sense, in terms of the classical philosophies, the one that is most relevant to our world is anarchism.[3]

The anarchic impact of the information economy is something that I first became aware of in 1997 when researching the issue of Intranets and information exchange within companies. It seemed clear to me, and co-author Melanie Howard, that the information revolution was of little use unless people were provided with access to that information and empowered to use it. Yet, this had implications:

> Arguably, the price of allowing access to information that empowerment implies is a less controlled, even anarchic, environment too.[4]

The volatility implicit in the new economy has also been discussed by Carl Shapiro and Hal R. Varian in their book *Information Rules: A Strategic Guide to the Network Economy*.[5] Shapiro and Varian 'explore the underlying economic forces that determine success and failure in the Network Economy' explaining why such aspects as *positive and negative feedback* and *network externalities* are so important in shaping the economy of the future. The interconnections of the network economy make markets less stable. As they put it, markets are more 'tippy' – a factor that is probably enhanced by the inherent cynicism and disloyalty (in the form of readiness to change brands) of modern day consumers. Another reason why markets are potentially more tippy is that the popularity of a product and service can, in the network economy, be dependent on the number of users. As more people use the product so, in some markets, the value of the product increases (see Metcalfe's Law in Chapter 6). They argue that the rapid decline of Apple in the 1990s was an example of this phenomenon.

More recently, the 'tipping' theme has been picked up by Malcolm Gladwell in *The Tipping Point*[6] who analyses further how and at what time the critical moment is reached when an idea, fashion or behaviour suddenly takes off. His examples range from consumer goods, through criminal activity (the rapid improvement in crime rates in New York in the 1990s) to the popularity of children's TV programmes. But Gladwell's most important contribution is to highlight the major underlying factors that influence the growth of an 'epidemic'. He identifies three 'agents' that are critical in the development of a tipping point: those individuals whom for whatever reason, are specially important in passing on news, information or whatever; what he calls the 'stickiness factor' – how memorable a 'message' is; and the environment at the time that the process starts – which may encourage it (as in the fuel protests in September) or discourage it (as in the lack of action on fuel in August).

How can companies operate and plan in an environment like this? Certainly, it is not easy and the temptation might be to give up now. But it might not be quite as bad as it seems, as there are some strategies that can be employed to mitigate the effects. First, within all this chaos there is, in fact, some order of sorts and thanks to the growth of computing power (and thanks to Moore's Law – see Chapter 6) there is now the ability, if not to predict the exact direction of the chaos, at least the potential scope of it. Second, citizen brands offer the prospect of managing better the inherent volatility in markets. Understanding this process and the role of citizen brands in a world of butterfly consumers is what this chapter is about.

THE EVIDENCE OF CHANGE

Beyond Britain's petrol crisis, what other examples of this phenomenon are there?

First, are examples of technology products where network effects (as outlined by Shapiro and Varian) have led to technically superior products losing out to inferior ones. These include Sony's Betamax video recorder that failed in the marketplace despite being technologically superior to the eventually triumphant VHS competitor standard. It also includes, as I have already noted, Apple's Macintosh computer that obtained market dominance in the desktop PC market with its innovative graphical user interface but lost out to the technically inferior 'Wintel' alliance of Intel processors and Microsoft Windows software. More importantly, when Apple started to lose market share it did so at an astonishing pace.[7] Other examples include Steve Jobs NeXT workstation and Digital's Alpha microprocessor chip which were, according to the *Daily Telegraph*, 'dramatically superior to their potential rivals'.[8]

Second, are fashion and related items. Malcolm Gladwell describes the way Hush Puppies changed from being a 'classic' but dying shoe brand to a hip fashion item in New York, all in the space of a very short time.[9] He also describes how a book by

Rebecca Wells – *Divine Secrets of the Ya-Ya Sisterhood* – having done moderately well in 1996 suddenly saw exploding sales growth a year later. Paul Ormerod in his book *Butterfly Economics*[10] discusses the processes by which one film stacked full of box office stars bombs out, while another is a huge success.

The third category is where new products, or new service delivery methods enter the market. Financial services currently provide some good examples here. In the early 1990s direct sales of motor insurance accounted for about 10 per cent of the total UK market. Some commentators claimed it was a niche segment and was unlikely to grow much further. Yet, direct channels now account for a significant proportion of motor insurance sales and other insurance is being affected too. By 1998 over two-thirds of consumers had bought their last new insurance (home, car or medical) via direct channels.[11] The change in market share by distribution channel had taken place over a relatively short (in traditional terms) period of time. In 1998, one of Britain's large and established insurance companies, Prudential, launched an Internet banking offer – one of the first independent on-line banks. In less than two years it had over a million accounts and was challenging for leadership in the on-line banking market.

Another obvious area where this phenomenon is noticeable is when there is some catastrophe that hits a company. This might be a physical incident like *Exxon Valdez*, when an oil tanker ran aground in Prince William Sound in 1989, causing huge environmental damage or when Coca Cola had a problem in its Belgium bottling plant resulting in the contamination of some of its product. Or, it could be the result of other actions or proposed actions. Shell, intended to dump its Brent Spar oil exploration platform in deep water but after a vigorous campaign by Greenpeace had to scrap the plan. In all these cases, the companies were commercially affected and the impact on them was very quick and almost impossible to manage. Sometimes these 'catastrophes' can be self-imposed.

In the 1980s Ratners was a successful and growing high street jewellery retailer in the UK. Then Gerald Ratner, who ran his family's firm, made some now infamous comments[12] during a public speech about the quality of his company's products and the business's fortunes plummeted.

While it can be argued that in each of these instances special circumstances were at play, it is all consistent with the idea that consumer markets are becoming less stable, less predictable and more prone to wild fluctuations in fortunes.

DECREASINGLY LOYAL, INCREASINGLY MERCURIAL

Part of the problem, is that it seems that consumers are less loyal than they were in the past. Although difficult to prove definitively, research at Cranfield in the early 1990s suggested that shoppers were more fickle than they used to be.[13]

This might seem strange at a time when companies are investing more and more in loyalty programmes. But the vast majority of consumers are experienced – having been born or raised in the post-war consumer society. They are much richer too – with far higher degrees of discretion in what they can and cannot buy. This mix of experience and growing affluence (see Chapter 5) provides consumers with the psychological and financial ability to change if necessary – a factor further encouraged by the greater choice now available to them. In fact, few consumers are inherently loyal in the sense of having a deep degree of attachment to a company or brand. As many as 50 per cent change their degree of loyalty over the course of a year (see Figure 10.2) and most people are promiscuous in at least some markets – fewer than a fifth nearly always buying the same brand in the majority of markets they operate in.[14] Although many people may, in fact, tend to buy the same brand

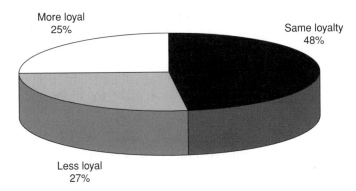

Figure 10.2   Less loyalty, more churn. Change between 1998 and 1999 to individuals' claimed loyalty to named companies (for example Coca Cola, Marks and Spencer, Barclays).

Source: Future Foundation/Consumers' Association/Richmond Events.

out of routine, boredom, lack of time or because they are over-whelmed by choice (see Chapter 7), they can change as a result of a negative experience or comment or through serendipity (seeing a new brand advertised, for example).

NEW MODELS FOR ANALYSING MARKET DYNAMICS AND MARKET SHARE

How then do we cope with all this volatility? How do we understand it?

Here, we can draw some help from the combined impact of new computing power and mathematical techniques developed for the fields of complex systems and biology. These allow us to develop models that are based upon the behaviour of individual firms and consumers and on the *interactions that take place between them*. Intuitively it is obvious, for example, that consumers in every market learn from each other's behaviour, learn from advertising, learn from events. These new models can be based on an acceptance that behaviour is not fixed, but is, rather – as I pointed out earlier – increasingly fickle thanks to increasing consumer experience, discretion and cynicism and the development of the network economy. More network connections make for more interactions and hence for more mercurial behaviour.

Paul Ormerod, in his book *Butterfly Economics*,[15] brilliantly demonstrates how such techniques can be applied to economic analysis. The core of the book focuses on how the learning from simulations of simple ant colonies can be applied highly successfully to social and economic situations. Ormerod argues that by using these techniques we can understand and explain a variety of outcomes that have consistently caused problems to classical economic theory. But the techniques can equally be applied to consumers and markets as Ormerod explains:

> Within the computer, an artificial world is created, populated by individual consumers. These individuals are given rules of behaviour which specify the conditions under which they become more likely to switch in and out of various products. Individuals need not be alike. All that is needed are some rules about how they behave.[16]

This new technique has been applied in a number of studies that have been able to explain otherwise less than obvious outcomes. Examples include the video recorder market I have already mentioned,[17] why financial markets are so volatile,[18] the inherent difficulty in predicting a film's success,[19] again as already mentioned, and why the business cycle is so impossible to anticipate.[20]

Roger Lewin and Birute Regine in their acclaimed book *The Soul at Work*[21] show how complexity science can be applied to the management and structure of organizations to improve understanding and performance.

WORD-OF-MOUTH AND PR DISASTERS – AN EXAMPLE

A simple example, from a deliberately simple model, helps to explain why 'epidemics' develop so much faster now, but also starts to provide clues as to the strategies companies can adopt to either exploit or counter the phenomenon.

In this example,[22] we start with a population of 250 people who are placed at random in a geographical space. These are shown as the circles in Figure 10.3 and the position of the circles can be considered to be, for this exercise, the home of the individual. Each person then has a number of 'connections', all with nearest neighbours – the lines in the figure. The idea here is to represent a past era where most people's friends, neighbours or colleagues would be geographically close by.

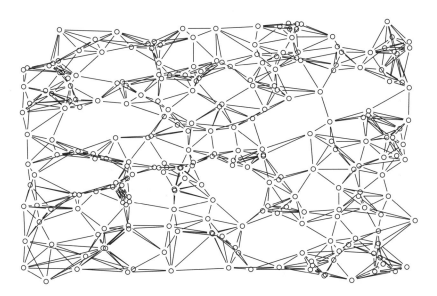

Figure 10.3 A network of the past: simulation.

Source: Future Foundation MathMatters.

What then happens when someone communicates with someone else – a word-of-mouth recommendation about a brand or new product, for example, or a warning about a health risk or the irresponsible or unethical behaviour of a company? We assess this by saying that an individual who has this knowledge has a certain probability of passing it on to all those she might be connected to *and* that the recipient has a certain probability of accepting or rejecting that advice. Another assumption is that over time people might 'forget' the piece of knowledge unless it is reinforced by hearing it again from someone else. Now we have a dynamic community where a piece of information will pass through it at varying degrees of speed depending on our assumptions about how likely someone is to pass on and positively receive the piece of information.

Figure 10.4 shows what happens over 20 time periods assuming that a small number of people in a particular geographical area

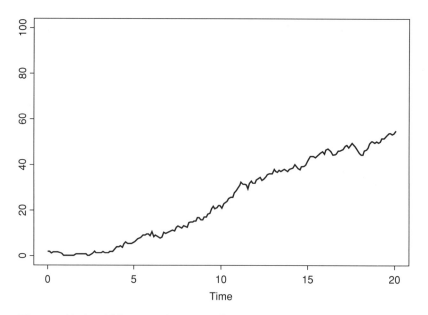

Figure 10.4 Old network – cumulative impact. Typical simulation.
Source: Future Foundation MathMatters.

are 'seeded' with the initial item of knowledge. It can be seen that it grows slowly and steadily until after 20 time periods (it could be days or weeks or months) over 50 per cent of the population have the 'news'. It should be noted that these simulations, as they are dynamic, will produce different results each time they are run but the figure represents a typical one for this situation.

But what happens if we increase the number of connections – as has happened in the network society – or the distance of the connections? The latter is important because now people are less bounded to a particular locality and will have friends, family and acquaintances who are more widely dispersed.

If we increase the number of connections by just 40 per cent but still keep these connections local we can see the effect on the spread of the 'epidemic'. Although it is hard to measure, it seems plausible that this sort of increase might match the increased

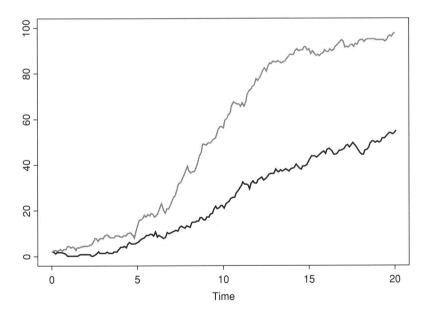

Figure 10.5 The impact of more connections. Simulations with different numbers of local connections.

Source: Future Foundation MathMatters.

number of connections that have arisen over the last 20 years or so as a result of changing social and work networks. If anything it is an under-estimate. Figure 10.5 then shows the impact of this. Just by increasing the number of contacts people have by 40 per cent we get a dramatic quickening in the spread of the rumour, recommendation or whatever. Now it takes only about 10 time periods before it reaches 40 per cent of the population.

But, it is not just that people have more connections in the network society, it is that they can also occur across great geographical distances – the radical transformation of time and space that I discussed in Chapter 6. Of course, such connections did exist in the past, but there are more of them now and news travels faster between them (an e-mail is a bit quicker than sea mail). As with biological epidemics which are known to spread much more quickly around the world with the advent of more and faster travel, so is the case with these word-of-mouth epidemics. It just requires one electronic connection to set up a new 'seed' of opinion on the other side of the world, which can then start spreading there. So, if we add just a few connections to those shown in Figure 10.3 but ones which link geographically distant points (like San Francisco to London) it has a big impact on the spread of the information.

Figure 10.6 shows what happens with just 14 additional connections – a very small number compared to the hundreds of links between the original 250 sample. Just by adding those extra few, but long, connections you get an even quicker spread of the 'epidemic'. Now it takes around seven time periods to reach 50 per cent of people. Whereas, increasing the number of local links by 40 per cent had a major impact, adding under 1 per cent of links, but making them long distance, has almost as dramatic an effect. This explains why it is an increasingly volatile consumer world but also provides some pointers on what to do about it.

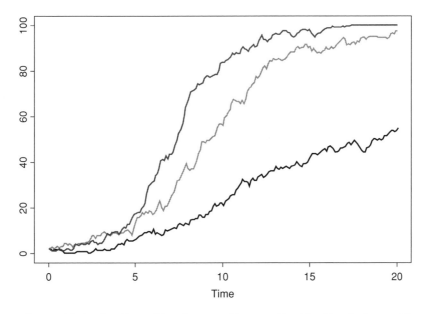

Figure 10.6 Small world – faster and less predictable. Simulations with different assumptions.

Source: Future Foundation MathMatters.

BUTTERFLY CONSUMERS AND CITIZEN BRANDS

While the arrival of butterfly consumers and butterfly economics poses real challenges for companies these new techniques for modelling these network systems do at least allow us to understand this uncertainty and plan for it.

An illustration of the use of the technique is contained in Lewin and Regine's book.[23] They show that by using complexity science you can understand why the management systems of some companies work and others do not. More importantly, they argue that embracing the concept of complexity, and implementing organizational systems that recognize it, leads to more successful companies. As Tom Peters says of the book:

Translate 'chaos theory' into usable business practice? Roger Lewin and Birute Regine do it![24]

Equally, these new models can be used to develop scenarios of likely outcomes given a range of possible strategic choices. By helping strategy development and providing a tool for rapidly analysing new situations as they arise, these techniques potentially offer significant competitive advantage. In this sense, uncertainty creates opportunity.

But being a citizen brand can help too and in three ways in particular. First, because a citizen brand is closer to society it is more likely to pick up signs of disruption earlier than other companies. Being a citizen brand is a bit like having an early warning system.

Second, as ethical consumption becomes more important, a citizen brand is more likely to get positive word-of-mouth recommendations. Finally, because of the bank of goodwill that has been built up (as I discussed in earlier chapters) these brands are likely to be 'stickier' – consumers are more likely to stick with them in the face of adverse publicity and the like.

These points relate to the general model of complex, network system as outlined in this chapter. From my discussion of this and the simulations I have shown, it is clear that there are a number of strategies to deal with the development of a butterfly economy. First, are those that affect the speed that information travels around the network. Already some organizations recognize this and use key opinion formers and/or new technology to promote the distribution of a product by word-of-mouth. This would include the currently popular idea of viral marketing. Second are those strategies that try to dampen network effects by decreasing brand switching. Here, most interest has been in loyalty programmes that increase the switching costs for consumers (by for example, providing monetary or other rewards to remain loyal which would be forgone if they took their custom elsewhere). The problem with the former is that you are continually trying to run faster to stay ahead of your competitors and, of course, it is inherently unpredictable – playing the chaos game can produce chaotic results. There is also the danger that you might be appealing to the most volatile set of consumers. The problem with the latter is that it has been shown not to work, or at least not to increase stickiness except in the very short term.

What are needed are more robust strategies for both sales and retention. For the first, reputation is critical – good product or service (as ever) is most important but increasingly there is likely to be an ethical or citizenship element too. For the second also, it is reputation, rather than loyalty gimmicks, that is likely to provide the brand stickiness that I discussed in earlier chapters as well as this one. For both, again, citizen brands are well placed. In an increasingly whirlwind, helter-skelter environment being a citizen brand will help provide smooth, lasting progress and a defence mechanism against the ups and downs of an ever more volatile consumer world.

BECOMING A
CITIZEN BRAND

CHAPTER 11

BECOMING A CITIZEN BRAND

*I*n this book, I have considered the overwhelming evidence that being a good corporate citizen is linked to commercial success and the reasons why this might be so. I have also discussed some of the history and the political and business backgrounds that have restricted a general and serious acceptance of this fact. Perhaps more importantly, I have also shown that for a whole range of reasons, citizenship is likely to become more important in the future. Thus, although it makes commercial sense to embrace it now, it is also a critical strategic issue.

Balancing short-term developments and long-term possibilities has always been one of the greatest challenges facing business. The dangers are obvious: look too closely ahead and you miss the long-term strategic developments you should be planning for now; look too far out and too strategically and you can become so blinkered that you miss the everyday, tactical decisions that are crucial for maintaining momentum, competitiveness and market share. Many corporate failures/disasters can be explained by errors in time-scale focus: too short, or too long.

Therefore, getting the balance right is critical to business success. Sometimes, it is appropriate to place more emphasis on the longer-term, strategic time frame; at other times, circumstances dictate a focus on a shorter time period. But the importance of citizenship is that it is not only a long-term strategic issue, but it can help when short-term tactical problems arise, as I have argued in the last three chapters.

So, what does being a citizen brand involve? At a general level it means placing society at the heart of the company, as I put it. This involves understanding not only the values, but also the concerns of employees, customers, investors and suppliers. But, in addition, it entails taking an active interest in local and wider communities and society at large – monitoring how well they are doing and the problems they face, and demonstrating that the company takes these issues seriously. Apart from just monitoring these issues – being outwardly focused, as I put it – what a company actually does will depend on the individual circumstances of the business: its history and previous activities and associations; the sector it operates in; and the particular concerns and interests of its people. Thus, some companies may focus on their workers and their families, others on the problems – like poverty, health or education – that face many third world countries. Some businesses may take an active interest in inner city poverty in the developed world, others in the environment.

A concern for environmental issues and animal welfare is part of The Body Shop's heritage, for example, and these areas are therefore an obvious focus for it. Cadbury's tradition of taking an interest in the local communities in which its workers live, means it has a historical link with helping to solve urban community and housing problems. Ford invests in education in the developing nations in which it is an employer, while Hewlett Packard has a community initiative aimed at helping the poorer countries of the world to benefit from new technology. Diamond producer De Beer has backed a campaign to eradicate polio – still a serious health problem in some of the areas of the world where it mines. Marks and Spencer, as a retailer, has a long tradition of working with the local communities in which its shops are based, and British multiple store Woolworths has provided money to staff to devise their own local community initiatives. Oil companies, not surprisingly, often focus on environmental matters, with BP's new logo and tagline 'beyond petroleum' underpinning its commitment to environmentally friendly technologies.[1]

FOCUS IS NOT CYNICAL

Although this focusing of citizenship activity could come across as a cynical exploitation of a company's market position, I do not believe it is. Rather, it highlights the complementarity and synergy between a given business and society that legitimizes the initiative and therefore improves the chances of its likely effectiveness. Looked at another way, there are some areas where it would be entirely inappropriate for companies to get involved. So, while Coca Cola can promote activities to help children, an alcohol or tobacco company cannot.

A particularly contentious area is involvement in sports and the arts. Research has shown that, when asked where they think companies have a role in helping out, the general public puts supporting the sports and arts at the bottom of a long list that includes education, the environment, working practices, fair trade and human rights.[2] Too often in the past corporate investment in these areas has reflected individual executives' interests rather than the broader concerns of their employees and customers. Sponsoring an opera company may be beneficial for its impact on opinion formers, the media and the intelligentsia, but it has little to do with corporate citizenship. The same would be true of investing in football teams in order to have your company or brand name displayed at the stadium or on shirts. This is pure marketing – a form of advertising – and not about being a citizen brand. The exception is, of course, where the initiative uses sport or art to reach or address a specific social or economic problem. Examples would include investment in inner city football pitches or sponsoring a performance arts programme for deprived children.

Although the emphasis of any citizenship activity may vary from company to company, it is important to recognize that a broader appreciation of, and concern about, what is going on in society will be important too. Only in this way, can companies reap all of the benefits of being a citizen brand that I have outlined in this book.

VALUES AND REPUTATION

In my introduction to this book I said the concept of citizen brands concerned three issues: corporate citizenship, core values and branding. My contention throughout the book is that, increasingly, companies will gain strategic advantage by building brands that embrace and encourage core values that have a citizenship component (in the broad sense in which I have described this). This does not just mean feeling guilty about a particular issue or problem, or giving money or some other form of benefaction. It means understanding society and the problems and issues that are engaging people – be they your customers, employees, shareholders, or whoever – around the world. It is about being outward-looking, not inward-looking; it is about actively participating in society rather than passively ignoring it.

By concentrating on consumer attitudes and behaviour, I have tried to demonstrate the importance of citizenship to branding. My argument is that the brand – and brand equity – will increasingly incorporate a feeling, a sense, of how in touch with the world a company or product is. And in a world where, perhaps paradoxically, I believe branding could become more important, this is clearly critical for the future success of a company.

But for citizenship to have an impact on reputation, for it to become truly part of the brand – its values and its equity – it must be *honest*. By that, I mean that the belief in citizenship and the activities associated with it must be sincere and exist in all parts of a company from top to bottom. For your employees, for your customers, for your investors, it's not just what you are saying or who you are saying it to, but whether the company really believes it too. As one chief executive said to me once, the 'drumbeat of values' needs to resonate throughout the organization.

TRANSPARENCY

Related to this point is the very crucial issue of transparency. In the new media environment, and in a world of a culture of fear and butterfly consumers, this is becoming ever more important. By transparency I mean being as open and honest as possible. This involves not only telling people what you are doing but, more importantly, providing transparent links to the company's beliefs, values, activities and behaviours – something that is now easily done with the new interactive technologies.

Transparency generates trust – since if you are not transparent it just looks like you have something to hide. More than that, transparency also means you have already established communications channels and mechanisms for better dealing with any public relations crises, for example, that may occur.

EMPLOYEES

Of course, one particular group of people who will expect an open dialogue are employees. They are a critical starting point for any business striving to be a citizen brand. For a citizen brand to succeed, employees at all levels must not only be aware of, and buy into, the values of the company, but feel validated and valued by it too. This is important for two reasons. First, as I showed in Chapter 1, employee satisfaction, and hence retention, is closely linked to customer retention and thus profitability.

Second, employees operate, in effect, as a company's 'window on the world' – a fact that is lost on some businesses. Workers have their own problems (childcare, low wages, concerns about crime, education or health) but they have their own ethical views as well. I showed in Chapter 2 that the confluence of these two factors determines the degree of concern individuals have about different issues. Knowledge of this is potentially very helpful for companies. Grocery retailer Tesco, for example, has grown to number one in the UK market as a result of a strategy focused on the customer. But in doing this, and in seeking greater flexibility from its employees to match changing customer needs, it then recognized that it needed to know more about its employees and their lives. This not only raised a whole range of work–life issues involving its staff, but also provided useful intelligence about society, family behaviour and shopping needs.[3]

As such, human resource departments can no longer be seen as stand-alone departments in the way they have sometimes been in the past. They need to work with both the marketing and strategy departments in the maintenance and development of the citizen brand concept.

KEEP EXECUTIVE PAY UNDER CONTROL

The most obvious place where there could be a dissonance between the values and practices of a business is in executive pay. Put simply, as I said in Chapter 1, excessive pay for senior managers does not sit happily with the idea of citizen brands. This is not because research suggests, as it does, that excessive pay is linked with poorer commercial performance (although you would have thought that would be a sufficient reason to keep pay under control). Nor is it, as such, because of some moral outrage at the obscene gap that is emerging between those at the very top of companies and most of its employees. The reason is that it is just not consistent with the concept of a company understanding, and being sympathetic to, the concerns and needs of society at large. It just grates.

An example makes the point. In the early part of 2000, Barclays Bank decided to close a number of its branches in rural areas. Personally, I can understand the pressure on high-street banks to do this as consolidation in the industry and the potentially disruptive impact of Internet banking will completely undermine previously-held cost and revenue assumptions about running a branch network. The problem was, as I noted in Chapter 4, that Barclays was doing this while it was advertising its ambitions and credentials as an international bank in its 'a big world needs a big bank' TV campaign. But worst of all, it also emerged at the same time that the company's senior executives were awarded massive remuneration packages. This created a huge amount of adverse publicity. At the bank's annual meeting, there was 'unusually high attendance and several demonstrations outside'[4] according to the *Financial Times*. One of the bank's senior managers, John Varley, received a grilling from John Humphries, one of the BBC's top current affairs presenters. Humphries started in a combative tone:

> It is an extraordinary way to run a bank, isn't it, Mr Varley? You close all these branches and then you award yourself potentially massive, massive amounts of money.[5]

Humphries continued in the same vein, always coming back to the huge amounts of money that Varley, and particularly Matt Barrett, chief executive of Barclays, were potentially going to receive. The estimated £15 million spent on an advertising campaign was being undermined by the minute. The money that was going to the senior executives was probably eclipsed by the loss of brand equity that the furore caused.

The problem is that it is unlikely that an executive who seeks a huge remuneration either understands or cares about those values that are embodied by the term citizen brands. My simple advice to companies and investors is to question whether prospective managers who want excessive remuneration packages (and this includes excessive share option schemes too) are really suitable to run a citizen brand company.

COMPETITION IS GOOD

Companies should also look at their strategies for market domination. Of course, it is a big temptation to work towards an effective monopoly in a market. And, for companies that would rather take the roller-coaster ride of regulatory investigation that it implies, this is an understandable strategy. But, if your ambition is to be a citizen brand, this is much harder in an oligopoly than in a competitive arena. Part of Virgin's success reflects its desire to attack cosy cartels and monopolies and it is rewarded with a great reputation among consumers. As I showed in Chapter 2, people are unlikely to view you as open, honest, truthful and trustworthy – key components of being a citizen brand – if you effectively control a market.

This creates huge problems for established companies in dominant positions who seek to soften their image and develop better relationships with the different communities they operate in as, for example, Coca Cola does (as I note in Chapter 2). How to execute that strategy for companies in this sort of position is a real challenge.

WHO SHOULD DEVELOP AND MANAGE THE CITIZEN BRAND STRATEGY?

The issue of corporate citizenship is of such great importance in terms of the vision, culture and strategy of a company that it should be the responsibility of the chief executive or someone (on the board) who reports directly to her or him. For all the reasons that I have outlined in this book, this is so important an issue and so critical to future success that it has to be at the heart of the company. Apart from all the other benefits I have outlined, it is an implicit part of the reputation-management function – an area of management that is increasingly being recognized as crucial. Charles J. Fombrun has summarized the importance of this nicely:

> Corporate reputations are strategic assets. Reputation management is an emerging discipline whose central tenet is that strong reputations result from conveying the genuine, distinctive values and personality of a company. The essence of building reputations does not lie in posturing, spin-doctoring or puffery. Rather, it presents reputation management as a source of competitive advantage – which makes it nothing less than enlightened self-interest.[6]

The fact that citizenship will not only increasingly be a part of branding, but that it also acts as a form of market intelligence (the 'window on the world' I referred to earlier), suggests that the citizen brand project would sit comfortably in the marketing department. This, however, would require marketers to embrace a more strategic role than some currently do and to look beyond short-term sales targets and fancy, awareness-raising advertising campaigns. This is a strategic marketing role, which is why it really should be the responsibility of the CEO.

CITIZEN BRAND IS NOT A SUFFICIENT CONDITION

One final, and crucial, point is that being a citizen brand is an increasingly necessary, but not on its own sufficient, condition for business success. I made this point in Chapter 1 and I make no apologies for making it again, even though it is so obvious.

Companies should not be diverted from everyday good business practice by the citizenship project – as a process it has to run alongside, often integrating with, the other aspects of management. Products and services have to be produced efficiently and to good quality and be cognisant of customer needs. Some of the commercial problems companies have had are not the result of their citizenship activities, but because they took their eye off the ball in one of these other areas.[7]

One of my own experiences with a client company makes the point. It involved a company that had a consumable product that was doing badly against its main competitor.[8] After sitting through a long presentation from the brand team about the advertising strategy and the core values to be promoted to the target market that had been identified, we were still at a loss as to why it was continuing to lose market share. Finally, I asked whether there was any taste difference between the two brands. Yes there was, in fact, I was told. In taste tests people preferred the competitor brand! My client's product was just not as good.

While this example does not relate specifically to corporate citizenship, the message remains relevant. If you do not have a good product, being a citizen brand in itself will not make many people buy it.

The other important area that companies need to concentrate on is innovation. Innovation is the 'big' management topic at the moment.[9] Being a citizen brand can help innovation as the company is less detached from society, culture, its customers and their values. And the combination of being a good citizen and being innovative is a winning one – indeed, these two factors represent the ideal attributes of a company in consumers' minds as I showed in Chapter 2.

WHO CAN BE A CITIZEN BRAND?

When I first started researching this book I was not at all clear that all companies would benefit from becoming a citizen brand – surely, some would not have the resources or inclination to embrace the concept. Others might have too much historical baggage to do it – a corporate culture that was just too dissonant with the idea. But, in the course of writing the book, I have formed the view that, as a concept, or perhaps more as a metaphor, it can apply to all businesses.

It is because it is *not* about benefaction and the use of resources that could be applied to other areas of business operations that it is generally applicable. It is because it *is* about an investment in the future, in stability, in research, in customers and employees that it has relevance for all. Some will do it more comprehensively and better than others (and reap the rewards accordingly), but there are elements that all companies can embrace. It is as much a frame of mind as a specific set of actions that can be implemented.

It is reasonable to suggest that given the tremendous financial struggles they often face, small and medium-sized businesses should be exempt from acting as good citizens. However, such firms are arguably closer to the environments they work in and the people (employees or suppliers) they work with. For them, therefore, corporate citizenship – particularly that with a local focus – may be very important. Not least, this is because it impacts on the reputation of the company in the local area, and hence word of mouth recommendations, which for many small businesses are an essential ingredient of success.

So, the prospect of being a citizen brand is open to every organisation. But it can only be obtained by those businesses who want not only to be successful but who also care about the state of the world they operate in.

A company may be tempted by the potential commercial benefits that being a citizen brand offers. But, if its managers do not care about excessive executive pay or child poverty or deprivation in the third world or the work–life balance of their employees – if they do not really care about any of these things at all – there is no point in pursuing the idea. The insincerity of any citizenship initiatives, the fact that they are not embedded in the core values of the organization, will nullify any potentially positive effects. Worse, it might even create increased cynicism and a reduction in brand equity. Companies that do not care cannot be citizen brands.

If, on the other hand, the corporate leaders accept that companies have wider roles and relationships with society; if they are concerned about their employees having a life outside work, the lack of opportunities for inner city ghetto children, the impoverishment of the third world, the environmental future of our planet; if they are concerned about any one of these or other social and economic issues, then they have a wonderful opportunity. Their company can become a citizen brand. It is not only the smart business call, but it is no less than their duty. They owe it to their shareholders, to their employees, to their customers, to society.

NOTES

INTRODUCTION

1 *The Responsible Organisation*, the Future Foundation/BT, 1997 (available from the Future Foundation).
2 Just because I use the term 'relationship' does not mean that consumers, for example, feel they have a 'relationship' as such with a company. Indeed, research shows that it is one of the least likely words consumers would use when talking about companies they buy from, even ones where they do so on a regular basis. (See, for example, *The Loyalty Paradox*, Brann, 1995.) Therefore, I use the term not in that personal way that individuals might use it, but rather to describe the broad links that exist between companies and individuals and other organizations, and the areas of mutual interest.
3 See, for example, Will Hutton's *Society Bites Back*, quoted in Chapter 3.
4 James C. Collins and Jerry I. Porras, *Built to Last*, Century Books, 1996.
5 The research was carried out jointly with Consumers' Association and Richmond Events and is discussed in more detail in Chapter 2.
6 Manuel Castells, *The Rise of the Network Society*, Blackwell Publishers, 1996.
7 A term first coined by sociologist Frank Furedi in his book *The Culture of Fear*, Continuum Publishing Group, 1997.

1 THE CASE FOR CITIZEN BRANDS

1 *Financial Times*, 17 October 2000.
2 *The Inclusive Approach and Business Success*, Centre for Tomorrow's Company, 1998.

3   *Introduction to Corporate Social Responsibility*, Business for Social Responsibility web site, www.bsr.org

4   *A New Vision for Business*, Committee of Inquiry report to the British Government, Summary Report, 1999.

5   Joel Schwartz, *Corporate Philanthropy Today: from AP Smith to Adam Smith*, Hudson Institute Working Paper, 1996.

6   According to McIntosh, Leipziger, Jones and Coleman, 'PIRC, pensions consultancy, said [of the Hempel report] that there were "many questions unanswered", and the Centre for Tomorrow's Company said that the committee had "missed a golden opportunity to broaden the approach to governance of British Companies". . . . It is clear that the Hempel Committee failed to meet the mood of the times.' *Corporate Citizenship*, Financial Times Pitman Publishing, 1998.

7   *Corporate Governance 2000*, PIRC, report in *Financial Times*, 20 November 2000.

8   'Three surveys on corporate governance', *The McKinsy Quarterly* 2000: Number 4. *Asia Revalued*, 2000.

9   *State of Working America 2000–2001*, Cornell University Press, 2001.

10 John E. Core, Richard W. Holthausen and David F. Larcker, *Corporate Governance and Firm Performance*, The Wharton School, University of Pennsylvania.

11 Ahmed Riahi-Belkaoui, *Corporate Social Awareness and Financial Outcomes*, Quorum Books, 1999.

12 Kotter and Heskett, *Corporate Culture and Performance*, The Free Press Macmillan Inc., 1992.

13 Quoted in *Introduction to Corporate Social Responsibility*, op. cit.

14 *Introduction to Corporate Social Responsibility*, op. cit.

15 Quoted in Collins and Porras, *Built to Last*, op. cit.

16 David Packard, *A Management Code of Ethics*, speech presented to the American Management Association, 1958 – quoted in *Built to Last*, op. cit.

17 Carly Fiorina, Commencement Address, Massachusetts Institute of Technology, 2000.

18 *Sunday Times*, 8 October 2000.

19 *Financial Times, Mastering Management Part Seven*, 13 November 2000.

20 Robert Waterman, *Frontiers of Excellence – Learning from Companies that Put People First*, Nicholas Brealey, 1994.

21 Business for Social Responsibility, op. cit.

22 Bill Catlette and Richard Hadden, *Contented Cows Give Better Milk*, Saltillo Press, 1998 – quoted by Business for Social Responsibility.

23 RSA Inquiry *Tomorrow's Company*, Centre for Tomorrow's Company, 1995.

24 *Financial Times*, 9 February, 1997. See also, Linda Bilmes and Konrad Wetzker, *People Factor: People Factor*, Financial Times Prentice Hall, 2000.

25 Business for Social Responsibility, op. cit.

26 Gary Hamel and C.K. Prahalad, *Competing for the Future*, Harvard Business School Press, 1994.

27 Randall L. Tobias, *The Best Days*, Address to shareholders at the annual meeting, Eli Lilly, 1995.

28   Lynda Gratton, *Living Strategy: Putting People at the Heart of Corporate Purpose*, Prentice Hall, 2000.
29   *Guardian*, 27 October 1999.
30   *Independent*, 30 June 1999.
31   Business for Social Responsibility, op. cit.
32   Author's personal discussions with the company.
33   *Guardian*, May 1997.
34   *Financial Times*, 21 April 1997.
35   *Does Improving a Firm's Environmental Management System and Environmental Performance Result in a High Stock Price?*, ICF Kaiser, 1997.
36   *Financial Times,* 3 July 1996.
37   Quoted in *A New Vision for Business*, op. cit.
38   Ahmed Riahi-Belkaoui, *Corporate Social Awareness and Financial Outcomes*, op. cit.
39   The Social Investment Forum, www.socialinvest.org
40   Quoted in John Hancock, *The Ethical Investor*, Financial Times Prentice Hall, 1999.
41   *Financial Times*, 27 June 2000.
42   Ibid., 24 November 1996.
43   Will Hutton, *Society Bites Back*, Industrial Society, 2000.
44   In *The Future of Brands*, Macmillan Press, 2000, Rita Clifton and Esther Maughan of Interbrand define a brand as 'a mixture of tangible and intangible attributes, symbolised in a trademark, which if properly managed, creates influence and generates value'.
45   Interestingly, Clifton and Maughan note how many of the contributors to their book 'talked about the increasing importance of brands as relationships', ibid.
46   I briefly discuss this issue further in Chapters 4 and 8.
47   Richard Branson, *Losing my Virginity*, Virgin Publishing, 1998.
48   *The Virgin Story*, company web site, www.virgin.com

2   BRANDS, CITIZENSHIP AND CONSUMERS

1   For fuller details of the project and its conclusions see the published report *The Responsible Organisation*, op. cit.
2   Richmond Events is an international conference and events organizer. Consumers' Association is the leading UK consumer organization and publisher of *Which?* magazine. The results of the research were presented at various Richmond Events conferences during 1998 and 1999 and a report of the research is available from the Future Foundation. See too, Michael Willmott, *Why Corporate Citizenship Pays*, Market Leader, Autumn 1999 and Michael Willmott and Paul Flatters, 'Corporate citizenship: the new challenge for business?', *Consumer Affairs*, volume 9, no. 6, November/December 1999.

3   *n*Vision is a subscription service from the Future Foundation that combines an extensive on-line data and analytic resource with workshops and briefings about future trends.

4   *The Responsible Organisation*, op. cit.

5   Gallup, 1999.

6   *The Responsible Organisation*, op. cit.

7   Ibid.

8   Background report available from the Co-operative Bank web site (www.co-op.co.uk) or Future Foundation.

9   Richmond Events, Consumers' Association, Future Foundation, op. cit.

10 Correspondence analysis is a statistical technique used to represent the results of a cross-tabulation in a two-dimensional map. The dimensions are statistical ones chosen to show to maximum effect the similarities and differences between the companies and adjectives. The way to read the map is by looking at which adjectives are closest to which brand – on the whole these are the adjectives that scored *relatively* more highly for that company rather than others.

11 *The Future of Brands,* Interbrand, Macmillan Press, 2000. Interbrand define brand value as the net present value of the economic profit that the brand is expected to generate in the future.

12 *Financial Times*, 17 June 1998.

13 Ibid., 27 March 2000.

14 Ibid.

15 *n*Vision, Future Foundation, op. cit.

16 In fact, I developed an index by scoring the responses to each question and adding them together. The result for each respondent was a score from 2 to 10, where a high score indicated a more 'ethical' stance.

17 In this instance, not only those agreeing but also those saying they could neither agree nor disagree were included. It seems to me that it is acceptable to interpret a lack of positive agreement with the statement as a degree of reticence about corporate behaviour. Certainly, the use of the word 'most' in the question may have made it harder for respondents to disagree directly since, for example, they might hold the view that many smaller, local companies are fair. Certainly, there is evidence that what antagonism there is, is directed towards larger, multinational companies who, with global consolidation, are likely to represent a smaller proportion of the total number of firms (see Chapter 9).

18 Richmond Events, Consumers' Association, Future Foundation, op. cit.

19 Respondents were given the following text and then asked whether they felt the named company operated in this way:

    Nowadays some people argue that companies need to recognise that they have an important role in society beyond just providing goods and services and employment for people. Indeed, it is suggested that it is in a company's own interest to be a good 'citizen': that is to recognise that it has a role to play in maintaining a happy and cohesive society. This could be through being a good employer, helping with social problems or actively participating in debate and analysis about social and economic issues (by, for example, getting its executives to work with government).

Although nearly 70 per cent of respondents thought companies generally should 'definitely' behave like this (and a further quarter 'possibly') only 13 per cent felt specific named companies did act 'a great deal' like this at present, with an additional 30 per cent saying they mostly did.

20   This is the classic statistical 'problem' of multicollinearity.

3   BEYOND PHILANTHROPY

1   David J. Jeremy *Capitalists and Christians,* Clarendon Press, 1990.
2   Ibid.
3   Gillian Wagner *The Chocolate Conscience,* Chatto & Windus, 1987.
4   Wilson, C. *The History of Unilever,* vol. 1, 1954.
5   *Detroit News,* 14 November 1916, cited in Collins and Porras, *Built to Last,* Century, 1996.
6   Robert Lacey, *Ford – The Men and the Machine,* Ballantine Books, 1986.
7   Gekko was the main character played by Michael Douglas in Oliver Stone's 1987 film *Wall Street.*
8   Francis Fukuyama, *The End of History and the Last Man,* Penguin Books, 1993.
9   Interview with a business leader, *The Responsible Organisation,* Future Foundation, 1997.
10   Naomi Klein, *No Logo,* Flamingo, 2000 – see also Chapter 9.
11   George Monbiot, *Captive State: The Corporate Takeover of Britain,* Macmillan, 2000 – see also Chapter 9.
12   *Policy Studies,* Policy Studies Institute, 1991.
13   Andrew Wilson, Director of Ashridge's *Managing Corporate Community Involvement* programme, writing in Ashridge's journal, *Directions,* October 1995.
14   *Society Bites Back,* Will Hutton, The Industrial Society, 2000.
15   Samuel Brittan, *Financial Times,* 1 February 1996.
16   Samuel Brittan, *Financial Times,* 8 July 1999.
17   Alastair Ross Goobey, *Financial Times,* 14 July 1999.
18   Mark Goyder, *Financial Times,* 23 July 1999. See also the *Tomorrow's Company Inquiry* report (mentioned in Chapter 1) which noted that 'For directors not to give appropriate weight to all the company's key relationships may well be a breach of their fiduciary duty'.
19   See, for example, John Elkington, *Cannibals with Forks: The Triple Bottom Line of 21st Century Business,* Capstone, 1997.
20   James C. Collins and Jerry I. Porras, *Built to Last,* Century, 1996.

4 A MODEL FOR CITIZEN BRANDS

1 In reality, of course, many people are sympathetic to all or most of these causes – and there is an undeniable left-of-centre stance to all this. But, the broad citizenship canvas does still bring together conservatives seeking corporate help with, say, animal rights or local arts funding and left-wingers campaigning to improve pay and conditions for workers or to counter human rights abuses.

2 ICF Kaiser report noted in Chapter 1.

3 Collins and Porras, *Built to Last,* op. cit.

4 See, for example, *Work-life Strategies for the 21st Century,* The National Work-Life Forum, 2000.

5 While I am an animal lover myself, I have to admit that given the choice of whether new medicines or cosmetics should be tested on animals or humans, I would choose the former. Perhaps, the protesters would prefer that the new products and treatments were not tested at all but this would lead either to potentially unsafe products being foisted on the public or no new developments at all – a form of extreme conservatism embodied in the Precautionary Principle that I discuss in Chapter 8. Whatever one's views on this, I could not condone the use of violence, either real or threatened.

6 *Who are the Ethical Consumers?,* Co-operative Bank, 2000.

7 Ibid.

8 *Policy Studies,* op. cit.

9 Executive interviews with business leaders quoted in *The Responsible Organisation,* op. cit.

10 Sir Iain Vallance and Sir Peter Bonfield in BT's Community Partnership Programme Report, *BT Cares,* 1997.

11 *Why do we have a Commitment to the Community?,* Marks and Spencer web site, www.marksandspencer.com

12 *Autocar India,* January 2000.

13 See, for example, Peters and Waterman's *In Search of Excellence,* HarperCollins, 1995; plus their individual works.

14 Gary Hamel and C.K. Prahalad, *Competing for the Future,* Harvard Business School Press, 1994.

15 Drucker is a prodigious writer and many of his texts are relevant here. For example, *Post-capitalist society,* Butterworth-Heinemann, 1993.

16 Viscount Leverhulme, quoted in David Ogilvy, *Confessions of an Advertising Man,* Atheneum, 1980.

17 Mike Hall, *How Advertisers Think Marketing Works,* British Market Research Society Annual Conference, 1991.

18 See, for example, Mike Hall, 'How advertising works: new steps on the advertising timeline,' Paper given to the APG Conference – Boston, 1998.

19 Whether this was the right advertising model to use when you are being accused of being insensitive to customers needs (because you are closing hundreds of local branches) is, to say the least, a moot point.

20   Mike Hall, 'How advertising works: new steps on the advertising timeline,' op. cit.

21   John Kay, *Financial Times*, 14 March 1997.

22   'How advertising impacts on profitability,' Leslie Butterfield, IPA, *Advalue Issue One*, September 1998.

23   The PIMS database was established in 1972 and now covers more than 3000 companies. It contains a range of data on each company covering financial, marketing and market characteristics. More details about PIMS are contained in *The PIMS Principles*, R. Buzzell and B. Gale, Free Press, 1987.

24   'How advertising impacts on profitability,' Leslie Butterfield, op. cit.

25   Ibid.

26   Alan McWalter, when Marketing Director at Woolworths.

5   PEACE AND PLENTY

1   Oliver James, *Britain on the Couch: Why are we Unhappier Compared to the 1950s – Despite Being Richer?*, Arrow, 1998.

2   Andrew Oswald, 'Happiness and economic performance', *Economic Journal*, 107, 1997.

3   Juliet Schor, *The Overworked American*, Basic Books, c 1991.

4   Juliet Schor, *The Overspent American*, Basic Books, c 1998.

5   John P. Robinson and Geoffrey Godbey, *Time for Life*, Penn State Press, 1997.

6   Robert H. Frank, *Luxury Fever: Why Money Fails to Satisfy in an Era of Success*, Free Press, 1999.

7   John P. Robinson and Geoffrey Godbey, *Time for Life*, op. cit.

8   Jonathan Gershuny and Kimberly Fisher, *Leisure in the UK Across the 20th Century*, Institute for Social and Economic Research, Essex University, Working Paper, 99-3, 1999. Also published in A.H. Kalsey (ed.), *British Social Trends: the 20th Century*, Macmillan, 1999.

9   Jonathan Gershuny, first published in *Prospect* magazine, but similar patterns are observable in Jonathan Gershuny and Kimberly Fisher, *Leisure in the UK Across the 20th Century*, op. cit. See also *Complicated Lives*, Abbey National/Future Foundation, available from the Future Foundation, 2000, and *The Millennial Family*, Boarding Education Alliance/Future Foundation, 1998. Note that Robinson and Godbey do not find any increase in child care time in the United States but that 'contrary to popular belief . . . both employed and non-employed women in 1985 spent just as much time in child care as those in the 1960s'.

10   John Seely Brown and Paul Duguid, *The Social Life of Information*, Harvard Business School Press, 2000.

11   Out of politeness for those in my fellow profession I will not name the specific organizations involved.

12   Jim Murphy is Director of Model Reasoning and an Associate of the Future Foundation and has developed the idea of Peace and Plenty for both his own work and for the Future Foundation. All the main tenets of the argument as outlined here were first developed and articulated by him. I, however, take responsibility for this particular description and some of the interpretations.

13   Source: National Statistics.

14   MORI, www.mori.com

15   The survey is carried out as part of the Future Foundation's *n*Vision service.

16   Melvyn Bragg, *The Soldier's Return*, Hodder and Stoughton, 1999.

17   David Gordon et al., *Poverty and Social Exclusion in Britain*, Joseph Rowntree Foundation, 2000.

18   For example, Ulrich Beck believes that 'Any attempt to create a new sense of social cohesion has to start from the recognition that individualism, diversity and scepticism are written into Western culture'. If cohesion is dependent on diversity and individual needs, then is a search for uniformity in income distribution a suitable strategy? Ulrich Beck, in *On the Edge*, edited by Anthony Giddens and Will Hutton, Jonathan Cape, 2000.

19   I see little evidence as yet of the development of a 'culture of envy' but it clearly will develop if income polarization continues unabated.

20   Source: National Statistics.

21   James Banks and Sarah Tanner, *Household Saving in the UK*, Institute of Fiscal Studies, 1999.

22   Abraham Maslow, *Motivation and Personality*, Harper, 1954.

23   Ronald Inglehart, *Modernization and Postmodernization*, Princetown University Press, 1997.

24   *The Millennium Poll on Corporate Social Responsibility*, Conducted by Environics International Ltd in cooperation with The Prince of Wales Business Leaders Forum and The Conference Board, 1999.

25   Respondents were asked to define a company's role: (a) 'Focus on making a profit, paying taxes and providing employment in ways that obey all laws' or (b) 'Do all this in ways that set higher ethical standards, going beyond what is required by law, and actively helping to build a better society for all' or (c) 'Operate somewhere between these two points of view'. The figure plotted in the graph is the proportion giving answer (b) minus those choosing (a).

26   *Who are the Ethical Consumers?* Co-operative Bank, 2000. These data are from the background report available from the Co-operative Bank website, www.co-op.co.uk

27   MORI defined 'post materialists' in the same way as Inglehart (op. cit.) did in his study that found increasing numbers of them over time.

28   John Gray, *False Dawn – the Delusions of Global Capitalism*, New Press, 1999.

29   Jeff Faux and Larry Mishel, in 'Inequality and the global economy', in *On the Edge*, edited by Anthony Giddens and Will Hutton, Jonathan Cape, 2000.

30   Shiva uses particularly strong language labelling globalization as 'environmental apartheid' and blaming it for 'the piracy of third world biological

and intellectual wealth'. Vandana Shiva, 'The world on the edge', in *On the Edge*, op. cit.

31   David Dollar and Aart Kray, *Growth is Good for the Poor*, World Bank, 2000.

32   Interestingly, research studies differ on whether employees actually feel less secure in their jobs. Recent analysis of British Household Panel Study data by the Institute of Social and Economic Research at Essex University suggests that during the course of the 1990s there has *not* been an increase in the proportion of workers feeling insecure in their jobs. Data available from the Future Foundation or ISER.

33   Charles Leadbeater, *Living on Thin Air*, Viking, 1999.

34   Mark Lilla, 'A tale of two reactions', *New York Review of Books*, 14 May 1998.

35   Philip Stephens, *Financial Times*, 6 November 1998.

6   BEYOND 'ENDISM'

1   In this chapter I concentrate on digital technology but, of course, there is another technological revolution around the corner – bio-technology and genomics. The impact of these could be even more important but the exact extent is far less clear at present. I do, tangentially, address some of the potential problems of bio-technology in Chapter 8.

2   Xerox's Palo Alto Research Center (PARC) is renowned for its research and development work. Seely Brown and Duguid note in *The Social Life of Information*, Harvard Business School Press, 2000 that it 'developed the elements of the personal computer' and specially, but not only, the concept of the 'graphical user interface' (GUI). The story of how Xerox was unable to exploit the GUI idea, allowing Steve Jobs from Apple to license it from PARC, incorporate it into Apple's Macintosh computer and change the face of the PC 'desktop', has now entered folklore.

3   John Seely Brown and Paul Duguid, *The Social Life of Information*, Harvard Business School Press, 2000.

4   To be honest, I have myself occasionally lapsed into such simplistic pro-nouncements. To be fair to myself and others, though, and although it is not always made clear, there is often an implicit, if not explicit, 'as we currently know it' qualification to these state-ments.

5   Although I couldn't agree with the general admonition of futurologists *per se*.

6   A particular favourite is Stewart Brand's book, *The Clock of The Long Now*, Phoenix Press, 1999 which, although it has a broader theme, provides a very coherent and compelling analysis of the importance of both Moore's Law and Metcalfe's Law. A good history of the microchip is provided in George Gilder's *Microcosm*, Simon and Schuster, 1989, while Bill Gates' take on the early days as described in *The Road Ahead*, Viking Books, 1995 is also interesting. Some of Gates' prognostications are not too bad either.

7   What became known later as Moore's Law was first postulated by Gordon E. Moore in a paper in the technical journal *Electronics* on 19 April 1965. Then head of electronics at Fairchild Camera and Instrument Corporation (later he was co-founder of Intel), Moore's paper noted that between 1959 and 1965 the number of components (transistors) that could fit on a chip had doubled every year. He predicted that this would continue, a prediction that was amended to doubling every 18 months following what in fact happened between 1965 and 1975. The prediction has remained remarkably accurate up to the present day. The impact is astounding, particularly as the acceleration continues. (Source: Stewart Brand, *The Clock of the Long Now*, op. cit.)

8   In mathematical terms, if V equals value and N equals the number of network users then the Law can be denoted as $V = N^2$. In reality, the real formula is $V = N(N-1)$ since in a net of ten users, each has nine others they can connect to – the total number of connections is $10 \times 9 = 90$. But if you double the number of users (to 20) each has 19 possible connections equalling a total of 380. A doubling of users has led to around a fourfold increase in connections (and hence value). Ten times the number of people equals roughly a hundred times the value; a thousand times the people gives around a million times the value. (Source: ibid.)

9   Ibid.

10   Throughout the rest of this chapter, when I refer to the uses of 'mobile phones' I sometimes use it as a generic term that includes other small portable devices – in other words including personal digital assistants or portable 'tablets'.

11   Anthony Giddens, *The Runaway World*, BBC Reith Lectures, 1999.

12   Stewart Brand, *The Clock of the Long Now*, op. cit.

13   Anthony Giddens, op. cit.

14   Quoted in Charles Leadbeater, *Living on Thin Air*, Penguin Books, 2000.

15   Manuel Castells, *The Rise of the Network Society*, op. cit.

16   Jonathan Gershuny and Kimberly Fisher, *Leisure in the UK Across the 20th Century*, Institute for Social and Economic Research, Essex University, Working Paper, 99-3, 1999. Also published in A.H. Kalsey (ed.), *British Social Trends: the 20th Century*, Macmillan, 1999.

17   Jonathan Gershuny, first published in *Prospect* magazine, but similar patterns are observable in Jonathan Gershuny and Kimberly Fisher, *Leisure in the UK Across the 20th Century*, op. cit.

18   See, for example, www.adbusters.com

19   I am thinking here specifically of the sociological theory of social exchange first proposed by Peter Blau in *Exchange and Power in Social Life*, John Wiley, 1964. Interestingly, the theory argues that *trust* is the critical element in social 'exchanges', reinforcing the importance of this in consumer and business exchanges too.

7   COPING WITH CHOICE

1   I wonder how much this view is – as in the discussion about 'peace and plenty' – a romanticized memory of the past. My own recollection from the 1960s is

of a sometimes poor, certainly inconsistent and occasionally even grumpy, service. Perhaps, though, my experience in London, where I was living, was not typical of the country at large, or, indeed, of other countries.

2 *Complicated Lives*, op. cit.

3 Ibid.

4 Ibid.

5 Source: A.C. Nielsen.

6 Ibid.

7 OFTEL suggest that you can assume that the average consumer now has at least three suppliers to choose from in the fixed line market. This is an absolute minimum, because issues arise about how to classify card operators who offer international discounts, re-sellers, etc. To the three fixed line operators, we add the four mobile suppliers. Source: *From Doormat to Digital: the Future for Bill Payments*, nPower/Future Foundation, 2000.

8 The research was conducted for the Future Foundation's *n*Vision service, op. cit.

9 *From Doormat to Digital: the Future for Bill Payments*, nPower/Future Foundation, 2000.

10 *Complicated Lives*, op. cit.

11 Ibid.

12 I am perhaps not completely objective on this point as one of my teenage children is a constant clothes shopper and continually complains about the lack of suitable clothes to wear.

13 *Complicated Lives*, op. cit.

14 Ibid.

15 Ibid.

16 *The Future of Brands*, edited by Rita Clifton and Esther Maughan, Interbrand/Macmillan Press, 2000.

8 SURVIVING A CULTURE OF FEAR

1 Reuters, 24 July 2000.

2 *New York Post*, 25 July 2000.

3 www.ci.nyc.nc.us

4 www.cdc.gov

5 Associated Press, London, 5 May 2000.

6 New York City Department of Health web site, www.ci.nyc.ny.us/html/doh/

7 See, for example, the European Commission's statement of its approach to, and guidelines for the use of, the principle in *Communication from the Commission on the Precautionary Principle*, Commission of the European Communities, 2 February, 2000.

8 Karl Popper, *The Logic of Scientific Discovery*, Hutchinson, 1959.

9 *Stewart Report*, Independent Expert Group on Mobile Phones, c/o National Radiological Protection Board, 2000 (also available at www.iegmp.org.uk).

10 See for example the well-publicized case of Lord Peter Melchett, Greenpeace campaigner, who led a group of activists to destroy a GMO test site. He and his fellow protesters were subsequently, and amazingly, acquitted of an illegal act.

11 Norman Levitt, Professor of mathematics, Rutgers University; author, *Prometheus Bedeviled: Science and the Contradictions of Contemporary Culture* – Author's notes from the Precautionary Principle Conference, op. cit.

12 *Financial Times*, 12 May 2000.

13 Author's notes from the *Precautionary Principle* Conference, op. cit.

14 Social Issues Research Centre, http://www.sirc.org/articles/beware.html

15 Freeman Dyson, *Imagined Worlds*, Harvard University Press, 1997.

16 'Chronic systemic pesticide exposure reproduces features of Parkinson's disease', R. Betarbet, T.B. Sherer, G. Mackenzie, M. Garcia-Osuna, A.V. Panov and J.T. Greenamyre, *Nature Neuroscience*, volume 3, no. 12, December 2000.

17 Interestingly, those who have argued against GMOs have not suggested this course of action as they are, on the whole, great supporters of organic farming. This points again to the political agenda underlying the debate about the precautionary principle.

18 Frank Furedi, *The Culture of Fear*, Cassell, 1997.

19 Ibid.

20 General Household Survey available from National Statistics.

21 British Crime Survey 2000, Home Office.

22 Barry Glassner, *The Culture of Fear*, Basic Books, 1999.

23 Ibid.

24 *Food Crimes*, Co-operative Wholesale Society, 2000.

25 *New York Times*, 30 July, 2000.

26 Stuart Sutherland, *Irrationality: The Enemy Within*, Constable, 1992.

9 SO-SO LOGO

1 Naomi Klein, *No Logo*, Flamingo, 2000.

2 Ibid.

3 George Monbiot, *The Captive State: the Corporate Takeover of Britain*, Macmillan, 2000.

4 Ibid.

5 Claire Short, quoted in the *Financial Times*, 26 September, 2000.

6 Attributed to Claire Short in the *Financial Times*, 26 September, 2000.

7 Kofi Annan, quoted in *Responsible Business*, The Prince of Wales Business Leaders Forum and the *Financial Times*, 8 November 2000.

8 Naomi Klein, *No Logo*, op. cit.

9 *Business Week*, 11 September 2000.

10 *n*Vision/Future Foundation.

11 The remainder, around a third of respondents, said they neither agreed nor disagreed. In the rest of this chapter, where I quote agree and disagree figures, the remainder will always be in the 'neither' category.

12 John Vidal, *McLibel: Burger Culture on Trial*, Macmillan, 1997; David C. Korten, *When Corporations Rule the World*, Earthscan, 1996.

13 Charles Handy, *Empty Raincoat*, Arrow, 1995.

14 Anthony Giddens, Analysis Programme, BBC Radio 4, February 1997.

15 The exact question wording here was 'Overall I think global capitalism benefits all'.

16 This was based on four different questions about attitudes to multinationals.

17 Laura Oswald, 'The place and space of consumption in a material world', *Design Issues*, Volume 12 (1), 1996.

18 Wendy Gordon and Virginia Valentine, *The 21st Century Consumer*, Market Research Society Annual Conference Proceedings, 2000. See also the work of the French school of sociology – for example, Pierre Bourdieu, Roland Barthes and Jean Baudrillard.

10 BUTTERFLY CONSUMERS

1 David Butler, *Financial Times*, 29 September 2000. Butler's figures represent the average across a range of polls so do not tally exactly with the MORI figures shown in the chart.

2 This term is derived from the title of Paul Ormerod's book *Butterfly Economics*, Faber and Faber, 1998.

3 Manuel Castells, *Wired Magazine*, November 1998.

4 *Inside Information*, a report for BT by the Future Foundation, 1997. Available from the Future Foundation.

5 Carl Shapiro and Hal R. Varian, *Information Rules: A Strategic Guide to the Network Economy*, Harvard Business School Press, 1999.

6 Malcolm Gladwell, *The Tipping Point*, Little, Brown and Company, 2000.

7 Carl Shapiro and Hal R. Varian, op. cit.

8 Bosses must learn from boffins, *Daily Telegraph*, 27 October 1999.

9 Malcolm Gladwell, *The Tipping Point*, op. cit.

10 Paul Ormerod, *Butterfly Economics*, op. cit.

11 Future Foundation, *Shopping Futures Study – Diary Study*, 1998.

12 He described some of the jewellery as 'crap'.

13 Knox and Dennison, *Profiling the Promiscuous Shopper: Evaluating Shopper Loyalty*, Cranfield University, 1993.

14 *The Loyalty Paradox*, Brann, 1995.

15 Paul Ormerod, *Butterfly Economics*, op. cit.

16 Personal correspondence with the author.

17 W.B. Arthur, 'Competing technologies, increasing returns and lock-in by historical processes', *Economic Journal*, September 1989 is one of the very earliest pieces of work in this whole area.

18 A. Kirman, 'The behaviour of the foreign exchange market, *Bank of England Quarterly Bulletin*, 1995.

19 A. De Vany and W.D. Wallis, *Economic Journal*, November 1996.

20 Paul Ormerod, *Butterfly Economics*, op. cit.

21 Roger Lewin and Birute Regine, *The Soul at Work*, Orion, 1999.

....

22 I am indebted to my colleague Michael Campbell who heads up the Future Foundation's MathMatters subsidiary who not only built these models but who has spent many hours discussing the concepts and issues with me.

23 Roger Lewin and Birute Regine, *The Soul at Work*, op. cit.

24 As quoted on Amazon's web site – www.amazon.com

11 BECOMING A CITIZEN BRAND

1 Some of these examples are also covered in either Chapter 1 or Chapter 4.

2 *The Responsible Organisation*, op. cit.

3 *Work–life strategies for the 21st century*, The National Work–Life Forum, 2000.

4 *Financial Times*, 27 April 2000.

5 Extract from BBC Radio 4's *Today* programme, published in the *Guardian*, 8 April 2000.

6 Charles J. Fombrun, 'The value to be found in corporate reputation', *Financial Times Mastering Management* series, 4 December 2000.

7 I gave the example of Marks and Spencer in Chapter 1.

8 For obvious reasons of confidentiality, I cannot identify either the specific product or the category.

9 See, for example, Gary Hamel's latest book *Leading the Revolution*, Harvard Business School, 2000.

INDEX